TO:

....

FROM:

....

DATE:

....

100 ADVENTUROUS STORIES

FOR BRAVE BOYS

MEMORABLE TALES OF MEN OF FAITH

GLENN HASCALL

BARBOUR **kidz**

A Division of Barbour Publishing

Scripture quotations are taken from the *New Life Version* copyright © 1969 and 2003. Used by permission of Barbour Publishing, Inc., Uhrichsville, Ohio 44683. All rights reserved.

Cover design and illustration by Jeff Crowther.

Interior illustrations by Scott Brown with colors by David Shephard, Christian Cornia, Jeff Crowther, Jesús Lopez, Joaquin Paris, Amerigo Pinelli, Ceej Rowland, and Karl West.

Published by Barbour Publishing, Inc., 1810 Barbour Drive, Uhrichsville, Ohio 44683, www.barbourbooks.com.

Our mission is to inspire the world with the life-changing message of the Bible.

 Member of the
Evangelical Christian
Publishers Association

Printed in China.

002288 1124 C8

CONTENTS

1. ABRAHAM 8
2. BROTHER ANDREW 10
3. AUGUSTINE 12
4. DIETRICH BONHOEFFER 14
5. WILLIAM BOOTH 16
6. SAM BRADFORD 18
7. DAVID BRAINERD 20
8. PAUL BRAND 22
9. DREW BREES 24
10. JOHN BUNYAN 26
11. WILLIAM CAREY 28
12. BEN CARSON 30
13. GEORGE WASHINGTON CARVER 32
14. DAN CATHY 34
15. STEWART CINK 36
16. DANIEL 38
17. DAVID 40
18. FREDERICK DOUGLASS 42
19. TONY DUNGY 44
20. JONATHAN EDWARDS 46
21. ELIJAH 48
22. ELISHA 50
23. JIM ELLIOT 52
24. EZEKIEL 54
25. RADAMEL FALCAO 56
26. CHARLES FINNEY 58
27. GIDEON 60
28. THE GOOD SAMARITAN 62
29. BILLY GRAHAM 64
30. DAVID GREEN 66
31. HEZEKIAH 68
32. PATRICK HENRY HUGHES 70

33. ISAIAH 72

34. JACOB AND ESAU 74

35. JAMES 76

36. JEREMIAH 78

37. JESUS 80

38. JOB 82

39. JOHN 84

40. JOHN THE BAPTIST 86

41. JONAH 88

42. JONATHAN 90

43. JOSEPH 92

44. JOSEPH, HUSBAND OF MARY 94

45. JOSEPH OF ARIMATHEA 96

46. JOSHUA 98

47. JOSIAH 100

48. ADONIRAM JUDSON 102

49. CLAYTON KERSHAW 104

50. KYLE KORVER 106

51. TRIP LEE 108

52. C. S. LEWIS 110

53. ERIC LIDDELL 112

54. DAVID LIVINGSTONE 114

55. MARTYN LLOYD-JONES 116

56. LUKE 118

57. MARTIN LUTHER 120

58. PETER MARSHALL 122

59. BART MILLARD 124

60. ROBERT MOFFAT 126

61. COREY MONTGOMERY 128

62. D. L. MOODY 130

63. MORDECAI 132

64. SAMUEL MORRIS 134

65. MOSES 136

66. GEORGE MÜLLER 138

67. WATCHMAN NEE 140

68. NEHEMIAH..142

69. JOHN NEWTON..144

70. NOAH...146

71. LUIS PALAU...148

72. JOHN PATON..150

73. PAUL...152

74. ALBIE PEARSON..154

75. JAMES W. C. PENNINGTON...........................156

76. PETER...158

77. ALBERT PUJOLS..160

78. NABEEL QURESHI.......................................162

79. NATE SAINT...164

80. STEVE SAINT...166

81. SAMSON..168

82. SAMUEL...170

83. FRANCIS SCHAEFFER...................................172

84. SHADRACH, MESHACH, AND ABEDNEGO..................174

85. KYLE SNYDER...176

86. SOLOMON...178

87. CHARLES SPURGEON....................................180

88. JOHN STAM...182

89. BILLY SUNDAY..184

90. HUDSON TAYLOR..186

91. ROBERT PRESTON TAYLOR.............................188

92. TIM TEBOW...190

93. WILLIAM TYNDALE......................................192

94. CARSON WENTZ..194

95. JOHN WESLEY...196

96. GEORGE WHITEFIELD...................................198

97. WILLIAM WILBERFORCE................................200

98. JOHN WYCLIFFE..202

99. BROTHER YUN..204

100. LOUIS ZAMPERINI......................................206

ABRAHAM
(GENESIS 12, 13, 17)

THE BIG MOVE

Have you ever sensed God asking you to do something that was too hard? Maybe you just didn't want to do it. Maybe it seemed scary.

Abraham was already old when God told him to move to a place he'd never even visited. God told Abraham, "Leave your country, your family and your father's house, and go to the land that I will show you. And I will make you a great nation. I will bring good to you" (Genesis 12:1–2).

Abraham knew where to find water. He knew where to find food. He knew his neighbors. He would miss his friends. He would miss his family. But because God asked, Abraham did the hard thing and moved.

The new land didn't look familiar. It was filled with people Abraham had never met. Everything was different.

God's promises may seem to take a long time to be fulfilled, but you can be sure that when God makes a promise, He'll keep it. Abraham had to wait twenty-five years for the baby boy God had promised. He named him Isaac.

Abraham was fearless. He trusted God enough to move to a new place. He was courageous enough to start a new life. He was brave enough to wait for God to give him a son.

If waiting seems hard, remember that Abraham had the same trouble. But in the end, God gave Abraham more than he hoped for. Be patient, because God has some great things planned for you too.

If we hope for something we do not yet see,
we must learn how to wait for it.
ROMANS 8:25

BROTHER ANDREW

(1928–2022)

SEEKING ADVENTURE

Do you like adventure? If so, you would probably get along very well with Andrew van der Bijl. Most people call him "Brother Andrew" because it's much easier to say.

Andrew was born in the Netherlands. His dad was nearly deaf, and his mom was disabled. All Andrew could dream about was a future that was active and filled with adventure. In the 1940s Andrew joined the military. When he was hurt in battle, he discovered a new future when he became a Christian during his hospital stay.

Andrew trained to be a missionary and then traveled to countries that didn't want Christians to visit. Because God was leading, Andrew could say to God, "Whenever, wherever, however You want me, I'll go. . . . I'll begin this very minute. Lord, as I stand up from this place, and as I take my first step forward, will You consider this a step toward complete obedience to You?"

Andrew was also known as "God's Smuggler" because he successfully took Bibles into countries where it was hard to get them. Government leaders didn't want them, yet the people needed them. Andrew would say that God did it. Andrew would be right.

Brother Andrew's story is a story of God's adventurer. He did what few other people felt brave enough to do. Andrew knew that the Bible is God's Word. He knew that if people could read it for themselves, they could meet God. He knew that if people met God, the world would change.

**All the Holy Writings are God-given and are made
alive by Him. Man is helped when he is taught God's
Word. It shows what is wrong. It changes the way of a
man's life. It shows him how to be right with God.**
2 TIMOTHY 3:16

AUGUSTINE
(354–430)

THANKS, MOM

Moms are pretty special. They take care of you, make good food to eat, and if you've been really good, they might take you to the park, zoo, or a friend's house. They might even bring homework to school if you forget it at home.

Augustine was born a very long time ago, and he had a very good mom. She followed Jesus and helped Augustine with his own faith. When Augustine was about your age, he was sent to a school where his mom couldn't help him make good decisions. There were no phones, internet, or online video chat. Augustine made his own choices, *and they were bad*. Augustine had once obeyed God because his mom wanted him to, but when she was no longer around, he struggled. You might know what that's like.

His mom would learn of Augustine's poor decisions, but by that time he didn't care. She begged him to follow Jesus, but he followed whatever interested him.

By the time Augustine was in his thirties, he returned to the Jesus his mother loved. He credits his mom's influence as part of the reason he sought Jesus. He read Romans 12–15, and that was the message God used to change Augustine's heart (read it yourself sometime). God used Augustine to influence centuries of Christians. God used a mom to influence Augustine.

The Bible talks about moms when it says, "She opens her mouth with wisdom. The teaching of kindness is on her tongue. She looks well to the ways of those in her house, and does not eat the bread of doing nothing" (Proverbs 31:26–27).

Children, obey your parents in everything.
The Lord is pleased when you do.
Colossians 3:20

DIETRICH BONHOEFFER

(1906–45)

HE SAID SO

Have you ever stood up for what was right and still got in trouble? It happens more than you think, and for many different reasons.

Dietrich Bonhoeffer was a pastor in Germany in the 1930s and '40s. He believed that God meant what he read in Galatians 3:28: "God does not see you as a Jew or as a Greek. . . . He does not see you as a man or as a woman. You are all one in Christ."

Since John 3:16 says, "God so loved the world that He gave His only Son. Whoever puts his trust in God's Son will not be lost but will have life that lasts forever," Dietrich thought it was wrong that the German government punished the Jewish people just because they were Jewish. Dietrich was certain that was not fair. *He said so.*

He knew the government didn't like what he had to say, which may be why Dietrich said, "There is meaning in every journey that is unknown to the traveler." He knew there was a purpose behind his longing for justice. He just didn't know where this path would lead him.

When the flowers were in bloom in 1943, Dietrich was arrested. Two years later he was killed. People remember him today because what he said was right, and what was done to him was wrong. Dietrich understood what some people forget: "One act of obedience is worth a hundred sermons." His life preached a powerful sermon: God loves all people, and all people are valuable to Him. That's very good news worth sharing.

What is important is to obey God's Word.
1 CORINTHIANS 7:19

WILLIAM BOOTH
(1829–1912)

PRAYER AND WORK

William Booth was not a typical preacher. He had a low growl in his voice, and he had a very long beard. He looked like a soldier. He even acted like one. William faced many struggles that might have caused him to give up, but with each new challenge he believed that God had something bigger for him. William once said, "Work as if everything depended upon work, and pray as if everything depended upon prayer."

If you guessed that William worked—*and prayed*—you're right. He prayed because he believed he couldn't do the work alone. He worked because he knew that obeying God was the right place to start.

When William was young, his family became poor. He had to leave school and begin work when he was only thirteen years old. Two years later, William was training himself to become a preacher. He discovered a friend who said he believed that the story of God's great rescue by sending Jesus to save humans was the greatest story anyone could share.

Each new ministry William worked with helped him learn what he needed to know to begin the Salvation Army. This ministry has always worked to make things easier for people who struggle. When people knew the Salvation Army cared about them, they listened more carefully to the message the Salvation Army shared.

People needed help, but they needed Jesus even more. That was the message William always wanted to share. William showed that passion when he said, "If I thought I could win one more soul to the Lord by walking on my head and playing the tambourine with my toes, I'd learn how!"

Remember to do good and help each
other. Gifts like this please God.
HEBREWS 13:16

SAM BRADFORD

(1987–)

CALM AND COOL

Some people get angry when things don't work out the way they want. That doesn't really describe Sam Bradford.

Sam played football. He expected to win. He scored points, broke records, and won awards. You would think that means he's a pretty intense guy. Many people who have played football with Sam think of him as calm and cool under pressure. He says there's something that helped: "My parents just realized that we were missing something in our lives. They realized that it was time for us as a family to start going to church."

That choice helped Sam learn about Jesus so he could accept His rescue. Jesus has become very important to Sam, and Sam shares his faith.

Sam didn't push his way to the front to get a football scholarship out of state. He grew up in Oklahoma, and the University of Oklahoma offered him a scholarship. He worked hard and became their quarterback. In his second year of college, he won the Heisman Trophy. When he graduated, he was one of the first players picked to play in the National Football League.

Sam quietly did his job. Colossians 3:23 says, "Whatever work you do, do it with all your heart. Do it for the Lord and not for men." Sam believes he has one boss, and he tries to do his best for God.

Sam isn't worried about the future. He knows that after he has done all he can, God still calls him His child.

Men become right with God by putting their trust in Jesus Christ. God will accept men if they come this way.
ROMANS 3:22

DAVID BRAINERD
(1718–47)

HE FOLLOWED HIS DREAM

Most people have dreams. You probably do too. There is something you want to be or something you want to do, but right now might not be the right time. There are always going to be things that seem to hold up a stop sign to your dreams.

David Brainerd had dreams, but his parents died and he became an orphan when he was only nine years old. He wanted a college education but was sent home when he became sick. He wanted to be a missionary, but if he was to be a missionary he would have to work while he was sick.

David coughed most of the time, but despite his serious illness, he worked with several Indian tribes in New York and New Jersey. He traveled more than three thousand miles by horse as a missionary. He preached, started a new school, and translated the Psalms for the people he worked with.

David didn't let being an orphan stop him from following his dream. He didn't let being kicked out of school stop him. He didn't even let his sickness stop him. David had perseverance. That means he stuck to his dream. David said, "We should always. . .glorify God and do all the good we possibly can."

For three years, David worked as a missionary. He wrote a journal that has been read by many. His story has encouraged men, women, and children to become missionaries. David died before his thirtieth birthday, but he followed his dream because his dream looked a lot like God's plan.

When we have learned not to give up, it shows we have stood the test. When we have stood the test, it gives us hope.
Romans 5:4

PAUL BRAND
(1914–2003)

GOOD PAIN

No one likes to get hurt. You stay away from pain as much as possible. Most people do. Paul Brand once thought pain was "God's one great mistake."

In the 1920s, Paul lived in India with his missionary parents. He saw people get sick. His father died. He didn't like to see people hurt. Maybe you think pain is a mistake too. Wouldn't it be better if people never felt pain?

Paul grew up to become a doctor. He was always interested in the pain that his patients felt. Some didn't feel pain, and that was a very big issue because it caused them to have even more problems. It may seem simple, but pain is God's warning system telling you that you've been hurt. Without pain, you might not know. You might never heal. You might not get help. Pain tells you to stop doing what causes pain and treat your wound. Pain actually stops you from hurting yourself even more.

Jesus said in John 16:33, "In the world you will have much trouble. But take hope! I have power over the world!"

If you hurt yourself, look for an adult to help you. When you hurt inside, you can ask God to help you. The psalmist wrote, "[God] heals those who have a broken heart. He heals their sorrows" (Psalm 147:3).

Paul Brand knew that pain can help you learn to trust God. He discovered that God didn't create pain to hurt you. Pain tells you when to stop doing the things that are hurting you.

"God will take away all their tears. There will
be no more death or sorrow or crying or pain.
All the old things have passed away."
REVELATION 21:4

DREW BREES

(1979–)

HE WINS

Do you know someone who seems to win *all* the awards and break *all* the records? It's easy to be jealous of successful people.

Drew Brees was the quarterback for the New Orleans Saints. Some people might be jealous of Drew. He has won more awards than he can probably remember. He has broken more records than you can probably name.

It might surprise you to know that Drew's parents divorced when he was young. His mom didn't stay close to her kids. Drew was discouraged as a teenager. He wondered if he had a purpose. It seemed as if everything that could go wrong went wrong.

That's when Drew gave his future to Jesus. He knew it was time to really follow Him. Drew would later say, "All I have to do is just give my best, commit the rest to Him. Everything else is taken care of. That takes the weight off anybody's shoulders. . . . You've got somebody looking out for you."

Drew could have been jealous of people who had both parents in the same house, or someone who was very close to their mom, or maybe even of people who just always seemed to know what God wanted them to do with their lives.

Spend your time wisely. Second Thessalonians 3:11 says, "Some are. . .spending their time trying to see what others are doing."

Do things that God wants you to do and you won't have time to be jealous of others. Learn from God, and you can learn to cheer when someone does a good job.

You still live as men who are not Christians.
When you are jealous and fight with each other, you are
still living in sin and acting like sinful men in the world.
1 CORINTHIANS 3:3

JOHN BUNYAN

(1628–88)

CAN'T STOP TALKING ABOUT JESUS

Telling someone about Jesus can be scary. You might think they won't understand. They could make fun of you. They could even call you names. You might want to give up.

When he was young, John Bunyan made fun of Christians. John lived in England in the 1600s. He wanted to learn more about Jesus after getting married. Jesus changed John's life. In fact, John became a preacher. He couldn't stop writing about Jesus. He couldn't help himself. He just had to share Jesus, even though some people didn't understand, made fun of him, and called him names. In John 15:18, Jesus said, "If the world hates you, you know it hated Me before it hated you."

John was so certain that God wanted him to tell others about Jesus, he said, "What God says is best. . .though all the men in the world are against it."

He was surprised that the people who seemed most against him were government officials. He was arrested twice for preaching and spent many years in jail. That's when he wrote one book and started writing another. Maybe you've heard of *The Pilgrim's Progress*. That was John's most famous book. Many people still read it even today.

John needed to share Jesus with others. He was brave and did what God wanted him to do even when it was hard.

Jesus loves you so much, and He's pleased when you think enough of Him to make sure other people know that Jesus loves them too.

Let your bodies be a living and holy gift given to
God. He is pleased with this kind of gift. This is
the true worship that you should give Him.
ROMANS 12:1

WILLIAM CAREY

(1761–1834)

GOD MAKES WHAT'S HARD, EASY

You might be able to do something that's easy for you but hard for others. It could be sports, video games, or reading. You may not know why it's easy for you, but it is. Maybe you feel proud that you can do something that isn't easy for other people. James 4:6 says, "God works against the proud but gives loving-favor to those who have no pride."

God is pleased when His children think more of Him and others than they do of themselves. It might have been easy for William Carey to think he was someone special. William knew how to make shoes and how to read, and he taught himself to speak many different languages. Most people he knew only spoke one language, but William learned to speak Latin, Greek, Hebrew, Italian, Dutch, and French, and then he learned even more languages.

William loved to work but seemed to know that God wanted him to be a missionary. He moved his family to India, where he worked for more than forty years. Yes, William worked. He took a job as a manager in a factory, he preached, and he became a professor. He did all this while still being a missionary.

It seemed easy for William, but his motto was "Expect great things from God; attempt great things for God." What seemed easy was just William doing the best for God because God wanted William's best. God helped William. He can help you too.

"Self-important" and "One who laughs at the truth"
are the names of the man who. . .is proud.
PROVERBS 21:24

BEN CARSON
(1951–)

FROM ANGER TO LOVE

It's normal to get angry when things don't go your way. You might get mad if someone is unkind to you. Anger seems to show up when life seems unfair.

Ben Carson was an angry boy. His father left his family when he was young. That wasn't fair. His mother was sent to the hospital because she was so sad. That wasn't what Ben had planned. He attended many different schools. Sometimes people were unkind. Things changed a lot for Ben, and he became angry. It was only when Ben let God help that he began to transform. He learned about forgiveness and compassion. Without anger, things became better for Ben.

God replaced an angry heart with one that could show love. Ben discovered that he wanted to help others instead of hurting them. As he grew up, he believed the best way he could help was to become a doctor. He was a good doctor. People noticed.

Have you ever wanted to give up? Maybe you thought that what God is helping you become isn't important enough. Ben understood. He thought the same thing. He said, "To THINK BIG and to use our talents doesn't mean we won't have difficulties along the way. We will—we all do. If we choose to see the obstacles in our path as barriers, we stop trying." Ben kept trying. You should too.

Ben wrote books and was asked to speak to large groups of people, and when he retired as a doctor, the president of the United States gave him a job. Ben Carson learned how to give a gentle answer in a sharp-word world.

A gentle answer turns away anger,
but a sharp word causes anger.
PROVERBS 15:1

GEORGE WASHINGTON CARVER
(1864–1943)

HE WANTED TO LEARN

Have you ever had someone say you're too small, too young, or too weak to do something? It can be annoying. They could be wrong.

George Washington Carver was born a slave and was kidnapped when he was just a week old. The kidnappers sold George's mother and sister, but George was rescued and returned to his slave owner, Moses Carver. George would take his last name from Moses. He was often sick and wasn't expected to live past twenty years of age. He wasn't supposed to become a teacher. It was annoying, and people were wrong.

George was the first black man to attend two different colleges. People learned to respect him. He was very wise about how to farm. George was also wise when it came to living life as a Christian. He taught eight virtues to his students: "Be clean both inside and out. Neither look up to the rich nor down on the poor. Lose, if need be, without squealing. Win without bragging. Always be considerate of women, children, and older people. Be too brave to lie. Be too generous to cheat. Take your share of the world and let others take theirs." George made sure his wisdom matched God's Word.

Today when people think about George, they think of him as a man who taught a lot about farming and the environment. George made sure that God was always welcome in all the things he was learning. He thought learning was something God wanted him to do, and he did it well.

He who listens to teaching is on the path of life, but he who will not listen to strong words goes the wrong way.
PROVERBS 10:17

DAN CATHY
(1953–)

EXAMPLES ARE IMPORTANT

Everybody needs a good example. You probably have one. It could be your dad, mom, grandpa, grandma, or neighbor. You learn from the people you follow. The things they do become the things you want to do. Examples are important.

Dan Cathy's example was his dad. Truett Cathy seemed to be able to teach Dan new lessons every day. Dan watched his dad build a company called Chick-fil-A. Dan watched his dad work every day, even after he celebrated his ninetieth birthday. Dan watched his dad treat every customer with respect and kindness. Maybe Dan's dad's best example was found in places such as 1 Timothy 4:12: "Show other Christians how to live by your life. They should be able to follow you in the way you talk and in what you do."

Today Dan spends a lot of his time visiting the restaurants his dad started. The employees learn what Dan saw his dad do. People have noticed.

Have you ever wondered why being an example is so important? If you say that you're a Christian but are always grumpy and unkind, you can find a better example in 1 Thessalonians 5:14–15: "Comfort those who feel they cannot keep going on. Help the weak. Understand and be willing to wait for all men. . . . Look for ways to do good to each other and to all people."

Why should you do that? Sure, other people watch you, but the real reason is that God asks you to. If He wants you to be kind, it's because He's already kind. Act like Him. Follow His good example.

"Do for other people whatever you would
like to have them do for you."
MATTHEW 7:12

STEWART CINK

(1973–)

THE STRUGGLE

You want to make good choices, right? Does it feel like the harder you try, the worse things get? Do you feel like giving up? Hang in there. You don't have to face your choices alone.

Stewart Cink understands struggle. As a golfer who wants to win tournaments, he said, "Golf is so difficult to master. It feels like the better you get, the farther you are away from perfection." The fact that you struggle may prove you want to make good choices.

Stewart didn't grow up in a big city. His parents weren't rich. He didn't plan on being a professional golfer. He just loved to play golf. He taught himself. Stewart won tournaments as a boy. He kept winning as an adult. But Stewart struggled. He didn't learn how to play from the best coaches. He wondered if he was good enough. In 2009 Stewart won the Open Championship against golfing favorite Tom Watson.

Stewart follows Jesus, so he appreciates the value of struggling. When tough days come, Stewart knows there's something to learn, and if God is the instructor, whatever he learns will be worth sharing. Stewart isn't perfect, but he spends time with the God who is.

The apostle Paul also understood struggle. He wrote in Romans 7:18–19, 21, 24–25, "I want to do good. . . . Instead, I am always doing the sinful things I do not want to do. . . . This has become my way of life. . . . There is no happiness in me! Who can set me free from my sinful old self? . . . I thank God I can be free through Jesus Christ our Lord!"

If we tell [God] our sins, He is faithful
and we can depend on Him to forgive us.
1 John 1:9

DANIEL
(DANIEL 6)

THE CHANGE IN DARIUS

Being punished for doing the right thing seems unfair. Maybe you know what that's like. Maybe you've asked God for help.

Praying got Daniel into trouble. King Darius was tricked into signing a law that said no one could pray or worship anyone but him. If they did, they would have to spend the night with lions as punishment. It seemed like a good idea to the king, but everyone knew that Daniel prayed to God morning, noon, and night. Darius forgot.

Daniel knew it was right to pray to God—not humans. He prayed just as he'd always done. That's when he was taken to the king who "tried to think of a way to save Daniel" (Daniel 6:14). The tricksters reminded the king he couldn't go back on his word. He was sad when they led Daniel to the lions' den.

The king stayed up all night, hoping Daniel had survived. He came to the den and called out, "Daniel, servant of the living God, has your God, Whom you always serve, been able to save you from the lions?" (Daniel 6:20).

God had saved Daniel! He sent an angel to keep Daniel safe. What seemed so unfair reminded everyone that God is amazing. King Darius said something wonderful about God: "He is the living God and He lives forever. His nation will never be destroyed and His rule will last forever. He saves and brings men out of danger, and shows His great power in heaven and on earth. And He has saved Daniel from the power of the lions" (Daniel 6:26–27).

"Do not be sad for the joy of the Lord is your strength."
NEHEMIAH 8:10

DAVID
(1 SAMUEL 17)

THE SHEPHERD'S SLINGSHOT

David would one day be the king of Israel. He spent most of his time with sheep. Three of his brothers became soldiers. They seemed embarrassed when David showed up with gifts from home. They seemed angry when he asked questions about the enemy.

Goliath was nearly nine feet tall. He challenged any man from Israel's army to come and fight him. If the soldier won, then Israel would win. If he lost, then Goliath's army would win. No one had taken Goliath's challenge. Then David, the shepherd boy, stepped forward.

Saul, the king of Israel, tried to help David get ready to fight. The king's armor was too big for someone as young as David. David had rescued sheep from bears. He had saved them from lions. David served God. God was bigger than Goliath. David chose to trust God instead of fearing Goliath.

David found five stones. He reached for his slingshot. He walked into the valley between the armies. Goliath made fun of him. David told Goliath that he served a big God. David said, "You come to me with a sword and spears. But I come to you in the name of the Lord. . . . For the battle is the Lord's and He will give you into our hands" (1 Samuel 17:45, 47).

That's what led to the moment when David made his slingshot whistle. One of his stones flew through the air and knocked Goliath to the ground. That day a shepherd boy defeated a warrior who threatened God's sheep. David knew that God was with him. God made David brave.

Rise up, O Lord! Do not let man win the fight against You.
PSALM 9:19

FREDERICK DOUGLASS

(1818–95)

HONEST FREEDOM

Having honest friends is nice. These friends do what they say and say what they mean. They care enough about you to make sure you hear truth. Friends like this can be hard to find.

Frederick Douglass was that kind of man. He was brave enough to tell the truth, and he expected others to do the same. Frederick was born into the hard life of a slave. He never understood why people could be so cruel to each other.

If people said they wanted slavery to end, Frederick didn't want them to stop saying it when they finished talking to him. Frederick found it was hard to find friends who would do what they said and who said what they meant— no matter who was listening.

Just before Frederick became a teenager, the wife of his slave owner taught him the alphabet. What Frederick learned only made him want to learn more. He shared what he knew, and then he learned even more. Within a year, Frederick came to believe in Jesus. The Bible he read said things like, "God does not show favor to one man more than to another" (Romans 2:11).

That was truth. That was honest. That gave hope to a young slave. Frederick knew that what he was learning had changed him. Many claim that when he became a man, he said, "It is easier to build strong children than to repair broken men." Maybe he remembered that it was wisdom and faith as a child that made him a man who knew that freedom should be for everyone, including broken men.

The honor of good people will lead them, but those who hurt others will be destroyed by their own false ways.
PROVERBS 11:3

TONY DUNGY

(1955–)

QUIET. ENCOURAGING.

Who encourages you? It could be family members, teachers, or friends. What makes them so encouraging? Maybe they support your dreams, believe in you enough that you feel confident, or pay attention to you so that you feel that your future has hope.

Tony Dungy writes bestselling books and hosts a radio show. He is a dad, and he was also a very successful football coach. He has won plenty of awards, but most people who have met Tony would say that he is a very good encourager. He surprised many people when he refused to yell at players and make them feel as if they had let the team down. He wanted to guide the team, not make them feel bad about themselves. He once said, "People look at me and see a calm, cool guy on the sidelines, and I want them to know that my Christian faith affects my coaching and everything I do." Tony's faith meant he believed what the Bible says in 2 Timothy 1:7: "God did not give us a spirit of fear. He gave us a spirit of power and of love and of a good mind."

Tony was so successful in coaching in the National Football League that many of his assistant coaches also became head coaches. Most took Tony's example to their new teams.

Tony didn't stop with football. He took his encouragement to places where people really needed someone to inspire dreams. Tony has worked with Big Brothers/Big Sisters, Boys and Girls Clubs, and other charities.

Tony was courageous in trying a new way to coach sports. God inspired him. Maybe you can encourage others too.

He who watches over his mouth and his
tongue keeps his soul from troubles.
PROVERBS 21:23

JONATHAN EDWARDS

(1703–58)

GOD MADE IT FOR US

God made the earth and everything in it. He made the sky and all you can see when you look up. He made air so you could breathe, water so you wouldn't be thirsty, and eyes so you could see all He made. And it was all good.

Jonathan Edwards spent a lot of time outside. He explored the height of trees, the depth of creeks, and the width of canyons. You might think he was just a boy who loved being outside, but Jonathan came to think of everything God made as a way to show His creativity, awesomeness, and wisdom.

Jonathan was very interested in spiders, the effects of light, and how God made vision so he could see all God's big and small creations.

The things Jonathan saw convinced him to say, "I will live for God. If no one else does, I still will." Jonathan followed God for the rest of his life. He was a preacher, he wrote books, and he was the president of a college, but God's wonder always found him applauding God for His creation.

Jonathan would have given God a standing ovation when he read, "Christ made everything in the heavens and on the earth. He made everything that is seen and things that are not seen. . . . Everything was made by Him and for Him" (Colossians 1:16).

When you're in a science class, taking a walk, or playing in the park, remember that God is a master Creator, and He is happy when you enjoy what He made. Jonathan did!

The heavens are telling of the greatness of God and the great open spaces above show the work of His hands.
PSALM 19:1

ELIJAH
(1 KINGS 17–18)

GOD'S WEATHER FORECAST

Imagine if it didn't rain for more than three years. Would you ask God for rain? What if He told you no?

The people wanted rain, but most of them would not ask God. They didn't believe He had the power to help. The people turned their backs on God. They found other things to believe in. Even the king turned away from God.

God wanted the people to seek Him even more than they sought rain. He sent Elijah with a long-term weather forecast for King Ahab. No rain. Lots of sunshine.

Elijah was fed by ravens in the wilderness. He rescued a mom and her son from starvation. He asked God to raise a boy from the dead. God answered each prayer for help. But the skies stayed blue, and the rivers became as dry as dust.

Evil King Ahab sought Elijah, but God protected him.

One day Elijah looked for the king and asked him to meet him on the mountain. On that mountain, Elijah proved that only God was worth following. Then when God was made famous, Elijah told the king to get off the mountain before the rain stopped him.

The sky was still blue. The king found it hard to believe Elijah, but Elijah believed God. He prayed and watched the sky turn from blue to gray to black. The rain brought life to the land. Yes, Elijah prayed, but God made it rain. He's the only one who could. It was spectacular.

We are sure that if we ask anything that He wants us to have, He will hear us.
1 John 5:14

ELISHA
(2 KINGS)

BIGGER THINGS

Elisha was the student of Elijah. He didn't mind small jobs. If Elijah needed water, Elisha got it for him. If he needed someone to carry something, Elisha carried it. If he needed company, then Elisha walked with him wherever he went.

God was getting Elisha ready to do bigger things. It wasn't long before people turned to Elisha for help. They knew that Elisha served God and that God helped Elisha.

The people weren't following God, but Elisha was teaching them, and they began to follow again. It was easy to believe that God was with Elisha. God did miracles through the prophet. He made poisonous water safe; he fed more than a hundred men with a few loaves of bread; he healed a Syrian soldier with a skin infection called leprosy; and he raised a child from the dead.

Elisha was willing to do what God asked, and he helped teach four different kings over fifty years. Elisha's life is a good example of what is written in 1 Peter 4:10: "God has given each of you a gift. Use it to help each other."

Jesus told a story that could have described Elisha when He said, "You have been faithful over a few things. I will put many things in your care. Come and share my joy" (Matthew 25:23).

God can use you too. Obey God in small things, and don't be surprised that He has bigger plans when you're willing to trust—and obey.

The Lord is my strength and my safe cover.
My heart trusts in Him, and I am helped. So my heart
is full of joy. I will thank Him with my song.
PSALM 28:7

JIM ELLIOT

(1927–56)

CONVINCED AND COURAGEOUS

Have you ever been so sure of something that no one could change your mind? That's the kind of confidence God wants you to have in Him. No one can rescue, love, or improve your future like God can.

Jim Elliot had that kind of confidence. He was sure God loved him when he was a boy, and he followed God for the rest of his life. Jim discovered things he liked to do. He was very good at giving speeches, acting, and writing.

But Jim needed to decide what he would do when he grew up. He became a missionary, saying, "It is [God's] business to lead. . . . It is [my] business to. . .follow."

Jim went to Ecuador. He wanted to work with the natives and share God's love with them. Jim worked for nearly four years when he learned that a cautious Indian tribe he'd been looking for had been found. He traveled with other missionaries, and they met the Indians along the Curaray River.

The tribe needed to know Jesus, but when the missionaries arrived, the tribe that did not want to be found killed Jim and his four missionary friends. Later the following was found in Jim's journal: "He is no fool who gives what he cannot keep to gain that which he cannot lose."

Other missionaries would return to the Indians, and this time the people listened. Many of those who had killed the missionaries became convinced that only God could rescue them, love them, and give them a future that didn't need hate. New life came to Ecuador.

Put away the old person you used to be.
Have nothing to do with your old sinful life.
EPHESIANS 4:22

EZEKIEL
(BOOK OF EZEKIEL)

BAD NEWS, GOOD NEWS

When someone gives you bad news, it can be hard to believe it. You want to think that bad things won't happen. But sometimes they do.

God gave Ezekiel the job of telling the people of Israel that they would be sent away from their homes. God made this decision because the people turned their backs on Him. Ezekiel had been given a hard job. Nobody wanted to believe him. God said in Ezekiel 33:30–31, "People are talking to each other about you. . . . They come and sit in front of you. . .and listen to the words you say. But they do not do them."

Ezekiel spoke for God, knowing that the people who wouldn't listen would be sent away, and that what he said to them might not change a thing. The people sinned for so long that they didn't believe God meant what Ezekiel said, but He meant every word.

Ezekiel did, however, have some good news to share: God's correction wouldn't last forever. A time would come when the people would come back home with a fresh choice to obey God. In Ezekiel 34:16, God said, "I will look for the lost, bring back those that have gone away, help those who have been hurt, and give strength to the sick."

Ezekiel had to be brave enough to tell the people of an entire country that they were not obeying, that God was paying attention, and that God corrects those who won't obey. He loved them too much to let them stay lost.

"I will give you a new heart and put a new spirit within you. I will take away your heart of stone and give you a heart of flesh."
Ezekiel 36:26

RADAMEL FALCAO
(1986–)

NOT ASHAMED

No matter what job you have when you grow up, you'll have the opportunity to tell other people about Jesus. You don't have to be a preacher. You could be a soccer player.

Radamel Falcao is that kind of guy. He's a great soccer player (some call it football), and his first nickname was *El Tigre* or "The Tiger." He has played in the World Cup and has been a part of many of the world's best soccer teams.

Radamel was born in Colombia and met his wife in church. The Bible has come to mean more to him than he believed possible. He said, "It's a manual full of teaching about what God put in place so that we could. . .be blessed here on earth. God is always there to help me."

If you think Radamel is keeping his trust in Jesus to himself, he said, "I want others to see the power of God at work in my life and recognize that this is possible for them too." He doesn't want to be known as someone who is a Christian at church and someone else the rest of the week. "I try to put all the different areas that make up my life into God's hands." When God has every part of your life, He can change you and draw others to join you.

Radamel is courageous in telling people about God and what He can do to change hearts and make futures better.

Do your best to know that God is pleased with you.
Be as a workman who has nothing to be ashamed
of. Teach the words of truth in the right way.
2 TIMOTHY 2:15

CHARLES FINNEY

(1792–1875)

TIME WELL SPENT

God wants you to do something for Him. He wants you involved. You could be someone who doesn't mind helping others, praying for someone, or showing kindness. But God wants something more.

Charles Finney was a preacher who had one thing he wanted to do for God: tell people about His Son, Jesus. Charles wanted people to accept rescue from Jesus so much that he said, "I could not spend my time with them unless they were going to receive the Gospel." Charles felt like he was wasting time if someone's future didn't change because of the good news he shared.

He believed what he read in 2 Timothy 4:2: "Preach the Word of God. Preach it when it is easy and people want to listen and when it is hard and people do not want to listen. Preach it all the time. Use the Word of God to show people they are wrong. Use the Word of God to help them do right."

That's just what Charles did. He wanted people to know that no matter what they thought, God was *always* right. Charles wanted his life to be filled with moments when he could share what he believed and show people that what he said about Jesus was exactly what he believed. He didn't want anyone to think you could say nice things about Jesus but never obey what He said.

Spend your time wisely. Share Jesus. Show the way He's changing you.

Your heart should be holy and set apart for the Lord God.
Always be ready to tell everyone who asks you why you
believe as you do. Be gentle as you speak and show respect.
1 Peter 3:15

GIDEON
(JUDGES 6–7)

JARS, TRUMPETS,
AND THREE HUNDRED MEN

The people of Israel were afraid of the Midianites, who were bullies. No one thought Israel could win a fight against them. The people of Israel did what the Midianites told them. God wanted the Israelites to follow Him, but they didn't listen very well.

God told the people, "I am the Lord your God. . . . But you have not obeyed Me" (Judges 6:10). Even when the people disobeyed, God loved them. He picked a man who was ready to help. God was bigger than the man's fear.

When God told Gideon to rescue the people, Gideon thought God had made a mistake because Gideon didn't consider himself to be a leader. But God never makes mistakes. God told Gideon, "Save Israel from the power of Midian. Have I not sent you?" (Judges 6:14).

God sent. Gideon went. Thirty-two thousand men showed up to fight Midian. Many were afraid. God told Gideon to send the fearful men home. Ten thousand stayed. God said there were still too many men. In the end, only three hundred men stayed to fight, but how could three hundred men win against the soldiers of an entire army? God had a surprise.

The men were given jars and trumpets. When the time was right, they broke the jars and blew the trumpets. Suddenly it was the Midianites who were confused and afraid. They began fighting against their own men. God was strong enough to take a small army and win a big battle. He used the courage of Gideon to inspire a few men to remember that when God is on your side, you can always be brave.

Trust in the Lord with all your heart, and do not trust
in your own understanding. Agree with Him in all
your ways, and He will make your paths straight.
PROVERBS 3:5–6

THE GOOD SAMARITAN
(LUKE 10:25–37)

BE THE NEIGHBOR

Jesus was a great storyteller. You can read His stories for yourself in the Bible anytime.

You should be kind, but who do you need to be kind to? Jesus knew you would want to know, so He told the story of the good Samaritan.

A man walked alone between Jerusalem and Jericho. The journey was dangerous because there were lots of hiding places for robbers. Some robbers jumped the man, beat him up, took his belongings, and ran away. The man was hurt so badly that he couldn't walk. He couldn't even call for help.

Two people came by. They noticed the man and saw that he was hurt. They should have helped him, but they didn't. Both men worked in the temple but made the decision to stay away from the injured man.

Just when the injured man thought there was no hope, the good Samaritan came by. Everybody was unfriendly to Samaritans. How could he expect someone who was considered an enemy to offer help? But the Samaritan stopped and took care of him.

This was the story Jesus told. He wanted everyone to understand that sometimes help comes from places you never expect and through people you never thought would show kindness. Probably the biggest lesson Jesus wanted you to know is that *you* can be brave enough to help someone even when other people won't. That's what Jesus does every day.

[Jesus said,] "Which of these three do you think was a
neighbor to the man who was beaten by the robbers?"
The man who knew the Law said, "The one who showed
loving-pity on him." Then Jesus said, "Go and do the same."
LUKE 10:36–37

BILLY GRAHAM

(1918–2018)

GROW WITH GOOD FRIENDS

Who do you admire most because of their faith in Jesus? It could be a pastor, family member, or friend. You might want your life to look a lot like theirs when you grow up. They might not even know they are examples of what it looks like to follow Jesus.

Maybe you've heard of Billy Graham. He is one of the most admired men in American history. He spoke with twelve presidents about his faith. He preached on television to more than a billion people. Many say that Billy introduced them to Jesus. He showed what it looked like to follow Jesus. Many followed.

Billy was born on a dairy farm in North Carolina. His family worked hard, and Billy seemed like any other boy. He liked to climb trees and do other things farm boys like to do. When he was sixteen years old, he went to a crusade featuring the preaching of Baptist pastor Mordecai Ham. And that night, Billy decided to follow God.

Many people inspired and encouraged Billy. Charley Young, Henrietta Mears, and Martin Luther King Jr. are just a few of the people who helped Billy discover what God wanted him to do. That was probably for the best since Billy originally thought he was going to be a scientist.

God has always asked people to help you because He doesn't want to leave you where you are. He has plans for your life, and there are people who follow Him who can help you learn what to do next to follow Him more closely.

What you have heard me say in front of
many people, you must teach to faithful men.
Then they will be able to teach others also.
2 TIMOTHY 2:2

DAVID GREEN

(1941–)

BE A DOER

Imagine that Christmas is next week. Your family knows what you want. You stare at the Christmas labels on the presents and wonder if you'll find what you want inside a box with your name on it. Now let's say you get two gifts with the instruction to give one away. Would that be easy to do?

David Green made that kind of choice for himself and his company, Hobby Lobby. All of the profit (the money he earns) is divided, and one-half goes to help people learn more about God, train students to serve God, and make God famous. David has given more than $500 million to help others. He believes in following James 1:22: "Obey the Word of God. If you hear only and do not act, you are only fooling yourself." Be a doer.

David's dad was a pastor. So were his brothers. David had a different idea. He served God by making miniature picture frames. That's how he started his company. From the beginning, he made sure that God could use what he earned to help others.

David's family also had a dream of creating a museum that was all about the Bible. And today the Museum of the Bible is open in Washington, DC.

This businessman knows that one day his company will close. That's why today he wants to serve the God who never leaves, never forsakes, and always welcomes those who choose to follow Him.

Each man should give as he has decided in his heart.
He should not give, wishing he could keep it. Or he
should not give if he feels he has to give. God loves
a man who gives because he wants to give.

2 CORINTHIANS 9:7

HEZEKIAH
(2 KINGS 18–20)

PRAY—DON'T STOP

Do you pray to God? Is it easy? Do you ever wonder if He's listening or if you're even saying the words right? Everybody feels that way sometimes.

Hezekiah was a king in Judah. If anyone had a reason to wonder if they were praying the right way, it was Hezekiah. His dad, Ahaz, was a terrible role model for his son and the country he was supposed to be leading. There was no place to go to worship God because Ahaz had closed the temple. The people could serve any god. This was really confusing. And this made God sad.

Hezekiah wanted to find a better way. He would become a better role model. He opened the temple, and the priests spoke only about the true God. The people were invited to follow God again.

Hezekiah was still learning about God when enemy soldiers came and said they were taking over. This is when Hezekiah learned more about praying to God. He read what God said in His Word. He wanted to speak to God about what his nation was going through.

There was no reason anyone should have expected the people of Judah to stay safe from their enemy, but God answered Hezekiah's prayer by protecting the people.

Praying to God is something you can do. It's something you *should* do. Philippians 4:6 says, "Do not worry. Learn to pray about everything. Give thanks to God as you ask Him for what you need."

When you need help, pray!

Let us go with complete trust to the throne of God.
We will receive His loving-kindness and have His
loving-favor to help us whenever we need it.
HEBREWS 4:16

PATRICK HENRY HUGHES

(1988–)

SURPRISED AND UNEXPECTED

Maybe you were born with a health issue that limits what you can do. Maybe you know someone who fits that description. You don't have to let it discourage you. Neither do they.

Patrick Henry Hughes was born without eyes, and he can't walk. He has never walked on a beach or watched a sunset. No one expected this.

He began to learn to play the piano when he was nine months old. He played in the marching band in high school, and his dad pushed his wheelchair. He's an author and a recording artist, and Patrick Henry loves Jesus.

Patrick Henry could have gotten mad, but he had a different way of thinking: "I see blindness more as an ability and sight more as a disability, because there are some people with sight who tend to judge others by what they see on the outside, but I don't see that. I don't see the skin color, the hair style, or the clothing people wear; I only see that which is within a person."

While some people thought Patrick Henry's story was sad, Patrick Henry says it was a great way to love people. When his parents asked God, "Why?" Patrick Henry said, "Why not?" When they didn't even feel like praying for their meals, Patrick Henry prayed. When their faith was weak, Patrick Henry's was strong.

Everything you think is bad is an important part of your story—and maybe it's the right story to encourage someone else when they're having a bad day. Maybe Patrick Henry's story encourages you too.

I am sure that God Who began the good work in you will keep on working in you until the day Jesus Christ comes again.
PHILIPPIANS 1:6

ISAIAH
(BOOK OF ISAIAH)

TRUSTED WITH GOOD NEWS

You might know a lot about Jesus, or maybe you're just beginning to learn. You may have committed your life to Jesus, or maybe you're considering it. You might tell other people about Jesus, or maybe the idea of sharing scares you a little bit.

Isaiah was one of God's messenger prophets. What makes Isaiah's story so special?

He was given the job of telling people about Jesus hundreds of years *before* Jesus was born. No other book in the Old Testament has more to say about Jesus and what He would do when He came.

Imagine being able to tell people about someone who will live in the future. You'd have to do a lot of guessing, but God told Isaiah about Jesus, and that was a big part of the message God asked him to share.

God must have known that telling people about the future would be hard, so He gave a promise in Isaiah 40:31: "They who wait upon the Lord will get new strength. They will rise up with wings like eagles. They will run and not get tired. They will walk and not become weak."

Isaiah would need to wait on God because he would need new strength. He had a big message to share, a big God to serve, and a big Savior to celebrate.

Many books in the New Testament remember the words God asked Isaiah to write. Not a lot has been written about Isaiah's life, but you can remember that when God asked Him to tell God's best story, Isaiah obeyed.

"Now go and write it down in front of them. And write it in a book, that it may be seen for all time to come."
ISAIAH 30:8

JACOB AND ESAU
(GENESIS 25–33)

FORGIVING A BROTHER

Brothers and sisters can be wonderful friends, but sometimes they might seem like enemies. They might get you into trouble, take some of your stuff, or laugh when you're having a bad day.

Jacob and Esau were brothers. Their parents, Isaac and Rebekah, played favorites. Mom liked Jacob, and Dad favored Esau. They were twins, but these two brothers couldn't stand each other.

Jacob tricked his brother to get something he really wanted, and Esau reminded his brother that Dad liked him best. When their dad was about to die, he blessed Jacob because Jacob tricked him into thinking he was really Esau. Jacob was happy that his dad blessed him and not his brother.

Esau had had enough. After his dad was buried, he said, "The days when I will have sorrow for the loss of my father are soon. Then I will kill my brother Jacob" (Genesis 27:41).

Jacob knew he had pushed his brother too far. So he ran away. He stayed with his uncle for many years. When he learned that Esau knew where he was, Jacob prayed, "Save me, I pray, from the hand of my brother, from the power of Esau. For I am afraid of him. I am afraid he will come and kill us all" (Genesis 32:11).

God had been doing something wonderful while the brothers were apart. When they met after so many years, Genesis 33:4 says, "Esau ran to meet [Jacob] and put his arms around him and kissed him. And they cried."

One of the best gifts you can give a brother or sister is forgiveness. It's a perfect gift to receive too.

"Forgive us our sins as we forgive those who sin against us."
Matthew 6:12

JAMES

(BOOKS OF MATTHEW, MARK, LUKE, AND JOHN)

FOLLOWERS ENCOURAGED

Each of Jesus' disciples had to decide what to do when Jesus said, "Follow Me." Then again, Jesus wants you to follow Him too. That's what being a Christian is all about—following Jesus. Have you made your choice yet?

James was one of the men Jesus invited on the adventure of a lifetime. James was a fisherman and the brother of another disciple named John. He was used to feeling the movement of a boat and the spray of sea waves. Pulling up the nets and tying down the boat came naturally to him. His life seemed simple, but it suited him. He wasn't looking for a new job.

But then one day Jesus said, "Follow Me." He wasn't asking James a question. He was letting James know He expected him to follow. James didn't know how to do that, but he said yes. In the years that followed, James heard stories, saw Jesus heal people, and ate food with God's Son. This was much better than mending nets and cleaning fish.

James was there at the beginning of Jesus' ministry; he was there at the last meal before Jesus was crucified; and he told people about Jesus after Jesus went back to heaven. He was one of Jesus' closest friends.

Everything about James' life changed after he met Jesus. God used James to start a change in the lives of people he met. That's exactly what can happen when you choose to follow Jesus. Get ready. Go!

Jesus spoke to all the people, saying, "I am the Light of the world. Anyone who follows Me will not walk in darkness. He will have the Light of Life."
JOHN 8:12

JEREMIAH
(BOOK OF JEREMIAH)

A MESSAGE THAT MUST BE SHARED

Do you believe God has something for you to do? You might think there are so many people on earth that God can't keep track of everyone, but the truth is that He can.

Jeremiah was one of God's messenger prophets, and God gave him a message. In Jeremiah 1:9–10, God told the nervous prophet, "I have put My words in your mouth. I have chosen you this day to be over the nations and the kings, to dig up and to pull down, to destroy and to throw down, to build and to plant."

Who would listen to Jeremiah? He thought he was too young. There was a good king named Josiah who was also young. Jeremiah helped teach the people what was in God's law. Josiah needed the help.

Years passed, and new kings came and went. As Jeremiah got older, his job became harder. No one wanted to hear God's message anymore. The new kings didn't want Jeremiah's help.

Jeremiah's family didn't like his message. The people in his hometown wanted him to stop talking about what God was doing. He was punished for speaking for God. Jeremiah cried because his message was true, yet no one was listening. Still, he couldn't stop telling people what God wanted. He had no peace unless he gave God's message.

God had given Jeremiah the hope he needed in Jeremiah 24:7: "I will give them a heart to know Me, for I am the Lord. They will be My people and I will be their God, for they will return to Me with their whole heart." That was just the promise Jeremiah needed.

Give all your worries to Him because He cares for you.
1 PETER 5:7

JESUS
(BOOKS OF MATTHEW, MARK, LUKE, AND JOHN)

GOD'S BEST NEWS DELIVERED

How do you fit the whole story about Jesus on one page? Simple: you can't. John 21:25 says, "There are many other things which Jesus did also. If they were all written down, I do not think the world itself could hold the books that would be written."

John wrote a book about the life of Jesus and knew there was more to share. Maybe the best we can do is create a highlight reel of the Son of God.

Ready?

Jesus was born in Bethlehem in a stable. His first visitors were shepherds. When He was twelve years old, He stayed behind in Jerusalem and taught the religious leaders. By the time He was thirty, He began telling people about changes God was bringing to the world. They learned that God loved *everyone*, not just a few. They learned that God was more interested in their hearts than their good deeds. They learned that He could heal and perform miracles and was very compassionate.

Jesus said He would need to die to pay for the sins of every person who has ever lived. His followers didn't want to believe something so terrible, but it happened just as Jesus said.

One Friday Jesus died on a cross, and on Sunday He rose from the dead. He paid for your sin, and He offers eternal life when you accept His gift of forgiveness and rescue.

When Jesus went back to heaven, He sent His Spirit to be with His growing family always. And that is why we call the story of Jesus "good news." In fact, it's the best news you could ever read.

God showed His love to us. While we were
still sinners, Christ died for us.
ROMANS 5:8

JOB
(BOOK OF JOB)

FAITHFUL ON BAD DAYS

What if your bicycle was taken from you? Would you miss it? Probably not, if you never rode it. But what if you had ridden that bike for as long as you could remember?

The Bible tells the story of a man who had everything taken from him. Job was a very rich man. He owned lots of land and animals, and he had many children. He loved God, but in one day everything was taken from him, even his health. Soon he was covered in painful sores. Job tried to understand, but he couldn't.

Friends dropped by to visit. They said Job must have done something to make God angry. Maybe he had made wrong choices. His friends made him feel worse. They were just guessing. They didn't make him feel any better about his situation.

Job asked God why everything had been taken from him. He couldn't remember doing anything wrong.

God asked this man in Job 40:2: "Will one who finds fault not agree with the All-powerful? He who speaks strong words against God, let him answer."

God made this world and everything in it. No one told Him how to do it. God didn't need to look through a suggestion box to make sure He was doing it right. Job didn't understand, but *nobody* can fully understand the God who said, "My thoughts are not your thoughts, and My ways are not your ways" (Isaiah 55:8).

Job had been impatient, but God was faithful. God would bless Job even more than before—with land, animals, and a new family.

God can be trusted on good days, bad days, and every other kind of day.

"Do not fear, for I am with you. Do not be afraid, for I am your God. I will give you strength, and for sure I will help you."
Isaiah 41:10

JOHN
(BOOKS OF JOHN, 1, 2, AND 3 JOHN, AND REVELATION)

FRIENDS FOREVER

If you could go back to any event in history, what event would it be? You might want to spend time with someone famous or be present for some important happening. Maybe there is a family member you'd like to see again.

John was one of Jesus' disciples, and if he could go back in time, he probably would have wanted to spend more time with Jesus. The Bible says that John was the disciple Jesus especially loved. After the other disciples had died, John was writing God's words.

John was there when Jesus brought a little girl back to life, when He prayed before the soldiers came to arrest Him, and when Jesus was crucified. John believed that Jesus was God's Son. He followed Jesus before He was crucified and after He rose from the dead, and John made sure other people knew about Jesus.

When John wrote the book of John, all the other books called Gospels (Matthew, Mark, and Luke) had already been written. Maybe he waited to write his book because he had such great memories of Jesus and wanted to make sure he shared the stories God needed him to share.

John didn't have to go back in time to be with Jesus because Jesus was always with him. John remembered what it was like to be with Jesus, and then he told everyone all about it. Why? Maybe he wanted you to have every reason to meet Jesus yourself. Jesus has always wanted to be your best friend. John knew what that's like. You can too!

"I call you friends, because I have told you
everything I have heard from My Father."
JOHN 15:15

JOHN THE BAPTIST
(MATTHEW 3)

SECOND PLACE

Some people seem to be born to do great things. Books are written about many of them. What if you were born to tell other people how wonderful someone else was? Would you ask for a new assignment?

John the Baptist was given just that kind of job—*before* he was even born. In fact, the messenger prophet Isaiah talked about John's job when he wrote, "Make the way ready for the Lord in the desert. Make the road in the desert straight for our God" (Isaiah 40:3).

That may seem like a strange job description, but John was supposed to make sure everything was ready so that when Jesus arrived, people would be ready to listen and follow Him.

When John started getting things ready, people started coming to hear him preach and see what he would do. They thought he was very interesting, and he was becoming famous. It's a good thing John remembered his real job, because when people start paying attention to you, it's easy to want them to keep paying attention.

When Jesus arrived, John knew he had done what he was supposed to do. He talked about Jesus and said, "He must become more important. I must become less important" (John 3:30).

Sometimes it can be hard to be happy for people when they seem important and you don't, but God gave John the job of helping people understand who Jesus was and then being happy that God's greatest message was finally being heard.

Trust your work to the Lord, and your plans will work out well.
Proverbs 16:3

JONAH
(BOOK OF JONAH)

GRUMPY DELIVERED

It's easy to think that someone has made so many mistakes that God should just give up on them. You might think someone is a lost cause. God *never* thinks of people that way. As long as a person lives, God shows kindness, mercy, and love.

You've read about messenger prophets like Ezekiel and Isaiah. They heard God's message and shared it. Jonah was a prophet who heard God's message, but he paid to get on a boat that was sailing in the opposite direction of the city he was supposed to deliver the message to. He didn't want to deliver God's message, so he tried running away from God. Big mistake.

God sent a fish that was large enough to swallow Jonah after he was tossed into the sea by the ship's crew. For three days, Jonah lived inside the fish. He had time to think. He changed his mind. Although he was grumpy, Jonah said he would deliver God's message.

The fish spit Jonah up on the shore in the exact place God wanted him to be. Jonah was afraid that if he delivered God's message, the people would obey and God would forgive them. Jonah didn't want that.

The people of Nineveh were mean, rude, and angry. Jonah would have been happy to see God punish them. He thought they deserved it. But God loves to show mercy, and Jonah had a very bad attitude. When Jonah delivered God's message, the people stopped being rude, mean, and angry. That was when Jonah *started* doing what the people of Nineveh *stopped* doing.

You should always be happy when God works a miracle in the lives of people He loves—and He loves everyone.

Be happy with those who are happy.
Be sad with those who are sad.
ROMANS 12:15

JONATHAN
(1 SAMUEL 20)

MAKE WAY FOR THE KING

Many people have a best friend. Maybe you do too. It's a very good thing to have a friend who really cares about you. Before David was the king of Israel, he had just that kind of friend.

Jonathan was supposed to become king after his father, Saul, died. But God had different plans. Jonathan agreed that God's plans were better. David, the boy who defeated Goliath, was anointed by the prophet Samuel to be the next king. Instead of becoming jealous of the shepherd boy, Jonathan became David's best friend.

David would come to play music for King Saul, and then he would spend time with Jonathan. Saul didn't want Jonathan to be friends with David, but when Jonathan grew up, David remained his best friend.

One day David heard that King Saul wanted to kill him. David asked Jonathan to warn him if this was true. Jonathan spoke with his father and learned that Saul was angry enough to kill David. Jonathan was sad when he told David the news: "'Go in peace. For we have promised each other in the name of the Lord, saying, "The Lord will be between me and you, and between my children and your children forever."' Then David got up and left, and Jonathan went into the city" (1 Samuel 20:42).

Maybe you have a friend you would help in any way you could. Maybe you've had a friend you miss because he moved. Maybe you've always wanted a very special friend.

Jonathan was a courageous friend. He thought more about friendship than he did about becoming king. There's something awesome about true friends.

A man who has friends must be a friend.
PROVERBS 18:24

JOSEPH
(GENESIS 37, 39–45)

BAD DAYS, GOOD GOD

Joseph was the great-grandson of Abraham, making him part of the family God had promised to Abraham. He was also his father Jacob's favorite son. Joseph liked being the favorite. Maybe it was when Jacob gave Joseph a special brightly colored coat that Joseph began to discover that his older brothers didn't like him very much.

Did they want to be Dad's favorite? Did they want their own special coats? Did they just want Joseph to stop bragging?

Being jealous sometimes causes people to make some very bad choices. Joseph's brothers were jealous. They decided they would take Joseph's coat. Then they made another bad choice. They sold their brother as a slave. The bad decisions didn't stop. They told their dad that Joseph had been killed.

Maybe you've never had a Joseph-sized bad day, but you've had bad days, right? You should know that God took the meanest trick Joseph's brothers ever played and turned it into a way to save many people from dying. God helped Joseph stay strong when *more* bad days came. When Joseph was sold as a slave, he was taken to Egypt where he would eventually work for Pharaoh, the mighty leader of Egypt.

Joseph made sure the Egyptians saved enough food, for God had said that a time was coming when they could not grow enough food. Because the people planned, they had enough to eat. Other people would also come to buy food from Egypt. One day Joseph's brothers came to buy food. Instead of being angry, Joseph praised God for making a plan that saved his family.

Whenever you have a bad day, remember Joseph's story. God can take your terrible day and turn it into something good.

Watch and keep awake! Stand true to the Lord.
Keep on acting like men and be strong.
1 CORINTHIANS 16:13

JOSEPH, HUSBAND OF MARY
(BOOKS OF MATTHEW, MARK, AND LUKE)

ONE REALLY BIG CHOICE

Being asked to do something that makes no sense can leave you feeling confused. Do you trust the one who asks? For instance, if a new kid in school is the one asking, you might say no because you don't know him very well. But if God is the one asking, the choice should be easier.

Joseph was a carpenter. He knew how to make wood smooth for creating furniture. He was used to the smell of cut wood. People bought the things Joseph made.

His life was simple. He worked hard. He was ready to get married to a girl named Mary. Joseph probably had ideas of what furniture he would make for their home together. That's when he heard something he wasn't expecting. Mary was going to have a baby. He was ready to call the whole thing off. He didn't want to hurt Mary, but this was a very big surprise, and he wasn't sure how to deal with it.

Then an angel came to visit Joseph and said, "Do not be afraid to take Mary as your wife. She is to become a mother by the Holy Spirit. A Son will be born to her. You will give Him the name Jesus" (Matthew 1:20–21).

Now Joseph knew what to do. He got married and helped take care of God's Son, Jesus.

When God asks you to do something, you can trust that saying yes to Him is the right choice. You can believe He will help you do it—even the hard stuff.

Those who know Your name will put their trust in You. For You,
O Lord, have never left alone those who look for You.
PSALM 9:10

JOSEPH OF ARIMATHEA
(JOHN 19:38–42)

KINDNESS INITIATIVE

Jesus died one afternoon. The sky was dark, and the hill where Jesus was crucified was silent. It was a strange and sad ending to His life. He healed and helped, fixed and forgave, taught and trained. *Now?* He was dead.

Joseph was a rich man from the city of Arimathea. He was a religious leader who noticed Jesus still hanging on the cross. He had an idea. Joseph made his way to see the governor, Pilate. He asked for Jesus' body so he could give Him a proper burial. Pilate agreed.

Joseph took the broken body of Jesus from the cross and placed it in Joseph's own tomb. It seemed the right thing to do.

Jesus didn't stay in the grave very long. He died on Friday, but by Sunday He'd risen from the dead. Imagine that. . .only needing to *borrow* a grave!

Joseph was called "good and just." He'd quietly followed Jesus, but when no one came to show respect to Jesus after He died, Joseph took action and did what needed to be done.

There would be no applause, award, or thanks from the people who watched Jesus die. But Joseph's kindness must have meant something pretty special to God, because his generous gift is mentioned in the books of Matthew, Mark, Luke, and John.

As you live God-like, be kind to Christian
brothers and love them.
2 PETER 1:7

JOSHUA
(BOOK OF JOSHUA)

BE AN EXAMPLE

It's nice to have someone teach you how to do things. Someday you can teach others what you've learned too. Joshua learned how to lead from Moses. He would need to know how to lead. When Moses could no longer lead the people to the land God promised to give them, Joshua led them to their new home. It wasn't easy.

God said He had a special way for Joshua to win a battle against a town called Jericho. God wanted the people to walk around the town walls. When the time was right, they would blow trumpets. You might not think something like that would help win a battle, but when the people obeyed, the walls of the city came crashing down. God's plans *always* work.

Joshua was a good example. Sometimes the people forgot that it was God who helped them. They thought it was a good idea to stop following God. Joshua told them, "If you think it is wrong to serve the Lord, choose today whom you will serve. . . . But as for me and my family, we will serve the Lord" (Joshua 24:15).

The best thing Moses ever taught Joshua was that the most effective leaders follow God. The best thing Joshua did was agree with Moses. The people finally came home. God brought them there. He gave Joshua the strength to help.

Joshua led by example because he learned by example. God is pleased when we're brave enough to show others what it looks like to follow Him.

"Have I not told you? Be strong and have strength
of heart! Do not be afraid or lose faith. For the
Lord your God is with you anywhere you go."
JOSHUA 1:9

JOSIAH
(2 KINGS 22–23:30)

THE RIGHT THING

You always have a choice to do good. Even when it seems like bad timing or you're tired, you can make good choices.

Josiah was six years old when his dad became king. His dad didn't make good choices. He died when Josiah was eight. That's when Josiah became king, but Josiah wasn't like his dad. He wanted to make good choices for himself and for the people who called him "King."

The new king was twelve when he had all the idols destroyed. By his midtwenties, Josiah gave instructions for God's temple to be repaired.

Nobody had visited the temple in many years, so a lot of work needed to be done. One day someone brought the king papers with writing on them. This was God's law. Nobody had read it in a very long time. Josiah had never seen it. When it was read, Josiah began to cry. The things he learned were things God wanted His people to do. No one was doing those things. *No one.*

King Josiah called the people of Judah together. Josiah "made an agreement before the Lord. He promised to follow the Lord and keep His Word and His Laws with all his heart and soul. . . . And all the people joined him in the agreement" (2 Kings 23:3).

Josiah decided he didn't want to follow the example of his father and grandfather. He wanted to follow God, and he wanted the people to follow God too. That was a great decision!

Before Josiah there was no king like him who turned to the
Lord with all his heart and soul and strength, obeying all
the Law of Moses. And no one like him came after him.
2 Kings 23:25

ADONIRAM JUDSON

(1788–1850)

HE WAS SMART; HE BECAME WISE

Do you know someone who is smart and isn't shy about telling you? That can get annoying, can't it?

Adoniram Judson was the smartest young man in his college. When he graduated, he had the highest scores of any student. He thought being smart was more important than trusting God. He had a lot to learn.

Eventually Adoniram wanted to be a missionary. If he thought that would be easy, he was wrong. He went to India to tell people about Jesus, but they made him leave. So he went to Burma (now called Myanmar), where his wife, Ann, died. Several of his children also died. He wanted the people of Burma to follow Jesus, but very few followed during his first few years as a missionary. Then? Adoniram was sent to prison. Being smart hadn't helped his situation.

Adoniram became courageous enough to believe God sent him to Burma. He once said, "If I had not felt certain that every additional trial was ordered by. . .love and mercy, I could not have survived." He learned to speak and write a new language. The people of Burma read the Bible in their language because of Adoniram. He wanted to be useful to God. God made him useful.

Adoniram was smart, but God is wise. He once thought he didn't need God, but God knew Adoniram would need Him.

More than two hundred years ago, Adoniram Judson made the decision to trust God. Today people still read the words he wrote, and they discover God's love. Before Adoniram died, he helped more than eight thousand people decide to trust God.

God can use smart people when they become wise.

For the Lord gives wisdom. Much learning and understanding come from His mouth.
Proverbs 2:6

CLAYTON KERSHAW

(1988–)

GET OFF THE BENCH

Clayton Kershaw had gone to church for as long as he could remember. He wondered if that made him a Christian. When he was in high school, he realized he needed to commit his life to Jesus. Most people he knew called themselves Christians. That's what he had called himself. But that is sort of like calling yourself a major-league player just because you watch baseball on television.

Clayton became a Christian and an impressive baseball player. He decided that if he was going to follow Jesus, he needed to get off the bench and really follow Jesus, the Coach.

Many people think Clayton is one of the best pitchers in baseball history. He plays for the Los Angeles Dodgers. Fans love him. More than that, God loves Clayton, and Clayton loves God.

He helps organizations that help people. He visited Africa and saw one ministry helping children. He decided to donate $100 for every strikeout he had that year. By the end of the season, Clayton would give more than $492,000 to help. He had a very good year.

Clayton learned something that you should know too. Ephesians 2:8–9 says, "By His loving-favor you have been saved from the punishment of sin through faith. It is not by anything you have done. It is a gift of God. It is not given to you because you worked for it. If you could work for it, you would be proud."

How important is Jesus to you? How has following Him made a difference in your life? How does the idea of getting off the bench to follow Jesus make you feel?

O taste and see that the Lord is good.
How happy is the man who trusts in Him!
PSALM 34:8

KYLE KORVER

(1981–)

MORE LIKE JESUS

Have you ever made a mistake and then told God, "I'll make it up to You"? Bad news. God doesn't allow makeup work; He doesn't accept extra credit. You can't make anything up to God. You can't work harder, share more, or be nice enough to erase a broken God-law.

Kyle Korver tried it, but he learned from that mistake. Before he became a star in the National Basketball Association, Kyle was a pastor's kid. He tried to do what he thought a good pastor's kid would do. He tried to be nice. He tried to pay attention. He even started a charity to help others when he was seven years old.

No matter how hard he tried, Kyle couldn't make God like him. Kyle needed to know the truth: *God already loved him.* Kyle needed to read Romans 11:6—and maybe you do too: "If they are saved from the punishment of sin because of God's loving-favor, it is nothing men have done to earn it. If men had earned it, then His loving-favor would not be a free gift."

Have you ever earned a gift? Of course not. If you earn something, it's because *you did something.* A gift isn't really a gift if you have to work to get it.

Helping others is something Kyle still likes to do, but now he has a better reason. He helps because he wants to be more like Jesus and not because he's trying to impress God.

All our right and good works are like dirty
pieces of cloth. And all of us dry up like a leaf.
Our sins take us away like the wind.
Isaiah 64:6

TRIP LEE

(1987–)

I WILL FOLLOW JESUS

Sometimes when people follow Jesus, they want to look, talk, and act like other Christians. The apostle Paul even said, "Follow my way of thinking as I follow Christ" (1 Corinthians 11:1). The truth is, you *can* follow someone else—*as long as they follow Jesus*. That's the important part.

Trip Lee is a rapper who is also a Christian. He's a pastor, and he has written a few books. Trip loves Jesus and wants to follow Him in every choice he makes. But Trip decided he wanted to be like Jesus—*by following Jesus*. If that sounds confusing, it's really not. Trip had heard God's good news from other people, but more than taking their word for it, Trip read the Bible for himself.

He discovered that to find his place in this world, he needed to find his place in God's world. In John 15:19, Jesus said, "If you belonged to the world, the world would love you as its own. You do not belong to the world. I have chosen you out of the world."

Trip's music honors what Jesus did and how He wants His family to act. Before Trip writes any new song, he spends time learning the things God wants him to know by reading the Bible. He doesn't want to make anything up. If he's going to be an example, then he knows he needs to understand what God says.

Spend time in God's Word. It will change your life and help you be a good example to others too!

"If anyone wants to serve Me, he must follow Me.
So where I am, the one who wants to serve Me will be there
also. If anyone serves Me, My Father will honor him."
JOHN 12:26

C. S. LEWIS
(1898–1963)

HIS FRIENDS WERE INKLINGS

If you play basketball, you play on a team. If you sing, you join a choir. If you're a Christian, you spend time with other Christians. And if you're C. S. Lewis, you're part of the Inklings.

C. S. Lewis wrote The Chronicles of Narnia series and many other books. He went to university in England and became friends with J. R. R. Tolkien (author of The Lord of the Rings series). They met other men who would all become authors. They called themselves the Inklings. Their friendship meant they could share ideas before writing them. Each person became a better writer because they became friends.

Ecclesiastes 4:9–10 talks about friends: "Two are better than one. . . . For if one of them falls, the other can help him up. But it is hard for the one who falls when there is no one to lift him up."

C. S. Lewis is remembered for the wonderful books he wrote—the stories that have inspired people and encouraged them to love God and follow Him faithfully.

God created you to have friends. God made you to be a friend. His Son, Jesus, said there was something every Christian needed to do: "You must love the Lord your God with all your heart and with all your soul and with all your mind" (Matthew 22:37); and then, "You must love your neighbor as you love yourself" (v. 39).

Jesus said these were the greatest commands ever. C. S. Lewis found his friends, and they wanted the best for him. You should find those kinds of friends too.

A friend loves at all times. A brother is born to share troubles.
Proverbs 17:17

ERIC LIDDELL
(1902–45)

THE RACE OF A LIFETIME

When you work hard, you might expect to be recognized or chosen first when a leader is needed. Would it be okay if you weren't picked first?

Eric Liddell was a very good runner. He was known as the fastest runner in Scotland.

The leader of his school said that Eric never seemed proud or demanding. He demonstrated what it looked like to follow James 4:10: "Let yourself be brought low before the Lord. Then He will lift you up and help you."

Eric went to the Olympics in Paris to compete in running. One of the events was happening on Sunday—and it was his best event. Would he run? It was an easy decision. Eric believed that God meant what He said in Deuteronomy 5:12: "Remember the Day of Rest, to keep it holy, as the Lord your God told you." Eric believed Sunday was this day. So he didn't run.

Instead, Eric raced another day and won. God was honored. A year later, Eric became a missionary in China. This was another way to honor God.

Eric knew what was most important. He said, "Each one of us is in a greater race than any I have run in Paris, and this race ends when God gives out the medals." That is the race of a lifetime.

Like Eric, when you live for Jesus, you're living your best life—and participating in the race of a lifetime!

We know that God makes all things work together for the good of those who love Him and are chosen to be a part of His plan.
ROMANS 8:28

DAVID LIVINGSTONE
(1813–73)

HE WAS WILLING

Nobody is an expert at everything. Some people know computers, while others know skateboards. Some know a lot about books, while others know how to paint. People who know some things always have other things they don't know much about.

David Livingstone knew that God had called him to be a missionary doctor. The problem was, there were people who weren't so sure. David didn't successfully pass the work he needed to do to become a missionary. If he hadn't been given a second chance, he would not have become a missionary. David wasn't thought of as a very good preacher. Most people believed he was a poor leader.

But David knew that the Bible was filled with men who were called by God, even though they had no idea what they were doing. God often used people who were untrained but willing to learn. This described how David felt when he took his first steps into Africa. He once said, "There is one safe and happy place, and that is in the will of God."

David wasn't always successful as a missionary. He wasn't always successful as a doctor. But he was willing to go where God sent him. The work David did changed the way people thought about slavery, helped the world understand Africa better, and brought medical help to the people of Africa.

This missionary made friends easily, and most tribal chiefs got along well with him. They didn't care how much David knew. They wanted to know if they could trust him.

If you are willing to do what God asks, then you shouldn't be surprised when He uses you in ways no one expected.

"With God all things can be done."
MATTHEW 19:26

MARTYN LLOYD-JONES

(1899–1981)

SPIRITUAL GROCER

Did you know that your plans can get in the way of God's plans? Did you know that God wants you to let Him make changes to the plans you have for your life? Does that seem unfair? If it does, you should know that no matter what you want to do when you grow up, God's plans will always be better.

Martyn Lloyd-Jones was the son of a grocer. It's not hard to imagine young Martyn delivering boxes and bags of groceries to customers of his dad's store. Maybe he thought he would take over the business and continue friendships with customers he knew by name.

Thankfully, Martyn was willing to follow God's plan. He said, "I am. . .grateful to God that He did not grant me certain things for which I asked, and that He shut certain doors in my face."

Martyn did try some of his own plans, but things got better when he turned around and followed God's plan instead. For Martyn, that meant he would become a preacher at the famous Westminster Chapel. For thirty years, Martyn taught the people of London. In a way, he was doing what he had done as a child. He was delivering "spiritual" food to people who had become his friends. And that spiritual food came from Jesus. Martyn worked for Him. He said, "The most approachable Person this world has ever seen was the Lord Jesus Christ."

[Jesus said,] "Anyone who hears My Word and puts his trust in Him Who sent Me has life that lasts forever. He will not be guilty. He has already passed from death into life."
JOHN 5:24

LUKE
(BOOKS OF LUKE AND ACTS)

THE EYEWITNESSES

You've probably watched television or listened to the radio, right? You've seen or heard someone talk about what they saw, heard, or experienced. This is called an eyewitness report. It's sort of like when a friend tells you what they did on vacation.

Luke gets the credit for writing the books of Luke and Acts in the Bible. He was a writer of history. But Luke wasn't one of the twelve disciples. He didn't travel with Jesus. He didn't see the miracles. Luke was a doctor who listened to people who'd seen Jesus, witnessed His miracles, and heard Him speak. He wrote down these eyewitness reports. Luke wrote the most complete report of Jesus' birth and made it clear that Jesus was God's Son and that He came to rescue you.

Doctor Luke traveled with Paul and witnessed what happened after Jesus rose from the dead. That's when he wrote the book of Acts. This book was all about the earliest church and how it grew. In Acts 22:15, Luke wrote what Jesus had told the apostle Paul: "You are to tell all men what you have seen and heard."

Maybe you've been an eyewitness. It's possible you've seen good things that God does. It could have been for your family, a friend, or someone in your town.

God would be happy if you did what Luke did—make sure others hear about how good He is. It doesn't have to be in a book. You could just use your voice.

How can they call on [Jesus] if they have not put
their trust in Him? And how can they put their trust
in Him if they have not heard of Him? And how can
they hear of Him unless someone tells them?
ROMANS 10:14

MARTIN LUTHER

(1483–1546)

WE ARE BEGGARS

Beggars used to be everywhere. They sat by the road and asked people to help them. They sat at the entrance to the city, hoping visitors would be kind to them. They would beg Jesus to heal them. And He often did.

Martin Luther was a well-known religious leader who thought every human was a spiritual beggar. Every person who ever lived needs God's help. Some will tell God what they need, and God will help. Some will need God's help but never ask.

God doesn't see you as a beggar. He has always loved you. To really understand how much you need God, Martin thought you should see yourself as a beggar who *knows* you need God's help.

You can't buy God's help, and you can't earn it. You can't expect God to force you to accept His help, but you can ask for it. He won't force you to take something you're not sure you want, but He wants you to trust that He offers the best help ever.

Not everyone liked thinking of themselves as beggars, and Martin found himself in trouble with people who disagreed. Martin knew that God said, "All men have sinned and have missed the shining-greatness of God" (Romans 3:23). When you come to God as a beggar who knows you need help, you can leave as one of His dearly loved children.

God has chosen you. You are holy and loved by Him.
Because of this, your new life should be full of loving-
pity. You should be kind to others and have no pride.
Be gentle and be willing to wait for others.
COLOSSIANS 3:12

PETER MARSHALL

(1902-49)

FREE TO STAND STRONG

Starting over in a place where you have never lived can be hard. Abraham had to do that. Maybe you have too.

Peter Marshall was born and raised in Scotland. In his twenties, he immigrated to the United States. Peter didn't have much money, but he did have a God-sized dream. He wanted to be a preacher.

He loved the idea of freedom and described what freedom was: "May we think of freedom, not as the right to do as we please, but as the opportunity to do what is right."

As a new citizen of the United States, Peter went to college and became the preacher he had always wanted to be. He moved to Georgia, and God used Peter.

After World War II ended, Peter was asked to be the chaplain (pastor) for the United States Senate. One of the things he said was, "Give to us clear vision that we may know where to stand and what to stand for—because unless we stand for something, we shall fall for anything."

Peter wanted to know what God had to say, and he wanted to stand for that above anything else. He could identify with Hebrews 12:1: "Let us put every thing out of our lives that keeps us from doing what we should. Let us keep running in the race that God has planned for us."

Peter left where he was for the place God wanted him to be. What keeps you from doing what you should? What keeps you from running in God's race?

"Look to the Lord and ask for His strength.
Look to Him all the time."
1 Chronicles 16:11

BART MILLARD
(1972–)

ALWAYS A FATHER

Bart Millard wanted a father who loved him. He wanted a father who encouraged him. He wanted a father who would listen. That didn't describe Bart's dad.

Bart wanted to be a football player to please his dad. While playing in high school, Bart broke both of his ankles. That ended any thought of making his dad happy.

Have you ever had to stop doing something you really liked to do? Did it feel like you were being punished? Did it make you sad?

God had something new for Bart to do—*sing*. He joined his high school choir and sang in his church. This was a surprise for Bart. He didn't think he could sing.

If he was going to sing, Bart wanted to sing Christian music, but something seemed to stop him. He was still very angry with his father, who didn't seem to love him.

Today when you listen to the music of MercyMe, you might think Bart Millard had a good childhood, but life was very hard for Bart. God walked with him, and Bart began to learn a lot about being a Christian.

Bart was forgiven by God. And Bart needed to forgive his dad. Forgiveness allowed Bart to write a song that you probably have heard—"I Can Only Imagine."

God loved Bart, and He listened to Bart. He encouraged Bart. Because God changed Bart, he could write songs that pointed hurting people back to God.

God has always been Father of the Year.

Bart was brave. He forgave what seemed unforgivable. He loved someone who seemed unlovable. He learned because he was teachable.

Who do you need to forgive? Will you do it?

God in His holy house is a father to those who have no father.
Psalm 68:5

ROBERT MOFFAT
(1795–1883)

NO NEED TO GIVE UP

Giving up is easy. Dropping out is natural. Showing up and holding on are harder. You might shut off a video game when you think you have no chance of winning. You might say, "What's the use of trying?" when homework gets tough. But God never gives up—and neither should you.

Robert Moffat was a missionary in southern Africa. He looked at the skies beyond his village and wondered about the people he couldn't see. They needed to know Jesus. Robert must have been sad when he said, "In the vast plain to the north I have sometimes seen, in the morning sun, the smoke of a thousand villages where no missionary has ever been."

So many people needed to know Jesus, yet Robert couldn't go where he saw the smoke. Robert always thought there just wasn't enough time to reach all the people who lived beyond his village. Maybe that's why he said, "We shall have all eternity in which to celebrate our victories, but we have only one swift hour before the sunset in which to win them."

Robert dedicated his life to reaching people in Africa for Jesus. His daughter, Mary, would become the wife of David Livingstone. David was also a missionary who made it possible for other missionaries to come to Africa. It was Robert who inspired his son-in-law to discover the people who started the fires that he saw from his African village. Robert never gave up on them.

Have you ever given up on something that seemed too hard? Ask God to help you be brave and to keep trying, no matter what.

Be happy in your hope. Do not give up when trouble comes. Do not let anything stop you from praying.
ROMANS 12:12

COREY MONTGOMERY

(19??–)

THE SCHOOL PROJECT

Nobody likes bad news, especially if it's about them. Bad news can come in many forms: losing a job, getting injured in an accident, or even learning you have a disease. That's what bad news sounded like to Corey Montgomery.

The doctor told him he had sickle cell anemia. Corey didn't know what that was, but he learned that it would cost thousands of dollars to treat and that many African Americans get the disease. He was African American. All that added up to bad news.

Corey didn't tell anyone about what the doctor said. He was a teenager. He wanted to act as normal as possible. When he was assigned a science project, he chose sickle cell anemia as his topic. He learned that being tired was normal. So was pain. His heart and lungs could be damaged. More bad news.

As Corey continued his research, he discovered that there was a possible cure using a bone marrow transplant. He began researching how to find someone whose bone marrow was like his. And his research saved his life! It's not often that a school assignment really does save a life, but that's Corey's story—and it was trust that helped Corey. He didn't just trust that there was a cure. He trusted that God loved him more than he hated the disease. Romans 8:29 says, "God knew from the beginning who would put their trust in Him. So He chose them and made them to be like His Son."

For Corey, bad news became good news. If you trust God, you too can know without a doubt that He'll be with you and continue to love you—no matter what hardships you face.

A man cannot please God unless he has faith.
Anyone who comes to God must believe that He
is. That one must also know that God gives what is
promised to the one who keeps on looking for Him.
HEBREWS 11:6

D. L. MOODY

(1837–99)

FROM SHOES TO SOULS

His name was Dwight Lyman Moody, but he went by D. L., and he didn't love God—at least not in the beginning. He wasn't a great student either. Edward Kimball was his Sunday school teacher who said, "I have seen few persons whose minds were spiritually darker than was [D. L.'s] when he came into my Sunday school class."

D. L. didn't seem to belong. He went to Edward's class because he was forced to. When he wanted to become a member of the church, officials made him wait a year. They didn't think he was ready.

D. L. sold shoes for his uncle. He couldn't find another job. He felt worthless. Even after he came to know Jesus, D. L. struggled. He wanted to be useful to God, but he didn't always make good choices, and he had trouble reading. He started a Sunday school class for children, but those who visited said he would often skip words and had trouble sounding out the rest. But Moody became a great preacher and started a church, three schools, *and* a publishing company.

God knows what you can become, and He invites you to join His family even when you've made some pretty bad choices. D. L. had no reason to think God could love him. People who met him didn't think he measured up. But D. L. learned to say, "Faith makes all things possible. . . . Love makes all things easy."

God's love turned a shoe salesman into someone who was used to encourage men in the Civil War, publish books that influenced millions, and preach sermons so people could find Jesus.

What do you think God has planned for you?

"We love Him because He loved us first."
1 John 4:19

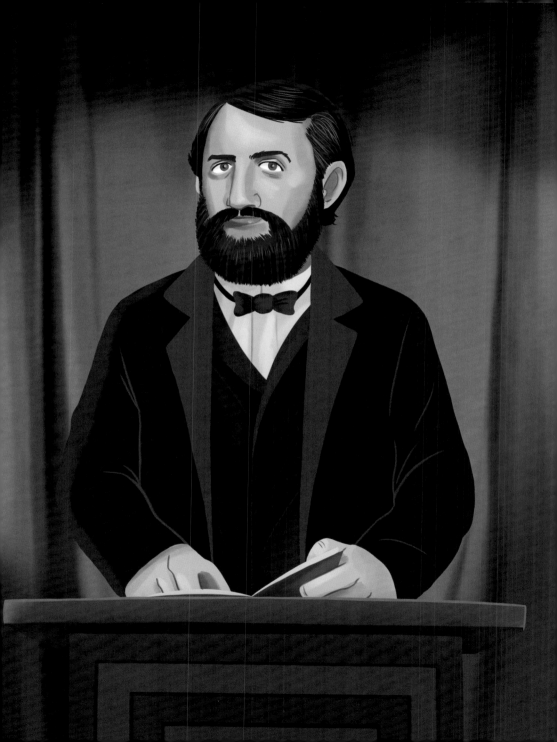

MORDECAI
(BOOK OF ESTHER)

EASY TO MISS

Have you ever read a story with a character you wanted to know more about? They weren't the star of the story, but they were super interesting.

Mordecai is that kind of character. He was the older cousin of Queen Esther. Maybe you know her story, but her cousin was a hero. He was often overlooked.

When Esther needed advice, she went to Mordecai. When someone was trying to hurt the king, Mordecai found out and kept the king safe. When a bad law threatened his people, Mordecai helped Esther understand what she needed to do.

There was one man who did not like Mordecai. Not even a little. Haman came up with a bad law because he wanted to punish Mordecai. Why? Mordecai would not bow to Haman. He refused. Over and over again.

One night the king was reminded that Mordecai had saved his life. The king ordered Haman to lead Mordecai through town and say, "This is being done to the man whom the king wants to honor" (Esther 6:11).

Honor? Why Mordecai? Haman wanted someone to lead *him* through town and say nice things. He wanted people to make fun of Mordecai. He didn't think it was right that he had to honor his enemy and miss out on a parade of his own.

Mordecai was a humble man who cared about his people and served God. He was easy to miss. Haman was a proud man who cared about what people thought of him and how he could become more powerful. Everyone knew him, but they didn't like his attitude.

Be like Mordecai. You'll never regret putting others first and following God's plan!

Nothing should be done because of pride or thinking about yourself. Think of other people as more important than yourself.
PHILIPPIANS 2:3

SAMUEL MORRIS

(1873–93)

THE SIMPLE FAITH OF A PRINCE

Kaboo was a Liberian prince who was taken prisoner by a nearby tribe. He was kidnapped and beaten nearly every day.

His family tried to free him, but they couldn't. One day Kaboo saw a bright light and heard a voice telling him to run. The ropes holding his arms together fell off. Although Kaboo was sick, he was free.

Kaboo was fourteen when he escaped. He found work at a coffee plantation. There he learned about Jesus. He was certain Jesus freed him. People needed to know Jesus.

This young man would become known as Samuel Morris. He worked on a ship to come to America. The very first night in America, Samuel shared what he knew about Jesus, and twenty people became Christians.

God was able to use Samuel to share His love. Samuel wanted to learn everything he could about Jesus so he could return to Liberia and share good news.

Samuel went to college, learned about Jesus, and led people to Jesus. When he was twenty years old, Samuel became very sick. He wouldn't make it home to Liberia. He wanted his family to know Jesus but said, "I have finished my job. [God] will send others better than I to do the work in Africa."

And God did. Many people were so inspired by Samuel that they volunteered to take the message he wanted to send home.

Samuel's simple faith in a big God led many people to follow his example and trust that God answers prayer. Do you have a simple faith like Samuel?

**[Jesus said,] "Teach them to do all the things I have told you.
And I am with you always, even to the end of the world."**
Matthew 28:20

MOSES
(BOOK OF EXODUS)

PLANNED AND PERFECT

Moses wasn't supposed to live. He was supposed to die as soon as he was born. But God had other plans. And God's plans are always perfect.

Moses was adopted as the grandson of Pharaoh. The plan was for Moses to live in the palace for the rest of his life. This was *not* God's plan. This plan was not perfect.

For forty years, Moses lived in the wilderness caring for sheep. This was where he was married. This is where his sons were born. He enjoyed the quiet. That would end, for God had a plan. Did you know His plan *was* perfect?

One day God asked Moses to leave the sheep behind and go back to Egypt. He would not be remembered as Pharaoh's grandson. He would not be given special treatment. God wanted His people to leave Egypt. He had a new home for them. That was His plan. Perfection.

Moses had been quiet and shy, but he became brave. Pharaoh was stubborn. God sent ten different disasters to Egypt, and Moses warned Pharaoh when each disaster was coming. All ten disasters came to Egypt before the people were allowed to leave.

The people lived in the wilderness for forty years, but God promised them a new land to call home. Because it was God's plan, it was perfect.

In the wilderness, God provided food, water, and the Ten Commandments for the people to follow. God took the courage of Moses, who thought he had already done the best he could, and He used that courage to save His people. That was God's plan. Wasn't it perfect?

Whatever you have planned for your life, you can trust that God's plan is *always* better!

As for God, His way is perfect.
The Word of the Lord has stood the test.
PSALM 18:30

GEORGE MÜLLER

(1805–98)

GOD MADE A WAY

If you needed your jeans washed, you probably wouldn't ask someone in school to wash them. You'd probably ask your mom or dad or someone who takes care of you.

George Müller understood that idea. You see, George ran several orphanages in London. Children who stayed with George always had meals, a place to stay, and a godly example.

If it sounds like George was a great guy, you should know that when he was young he stole money from his dad, cheated, lied, and gambled.

God changed George. The closer he got to God, the less interested he was in asking help from anyone else. He said, "If you walk with Him and look to Him, and expect help from Him, He will never fail you."

Without asking anyone for help, God brought George food, milk, and money for his orphanages when it was needed most. Once when he was traveling across the ocean to go to an important meeting, fog rolled in and the captain of the ship told him he wouldn't make it to the meeting. George prayed with the captain. When George asked the captain to look again, the fog was gone!

George lived every day knowing that if something could be done, it would be done because God would take care of it.

You might think the best way to do things is to work as hard as you can and then ask for God's help when it gets too hard. God wants to be given the chance to help in every situation. He will *always* handle things better than you can.

Answer me when I call, O my God Who is right and good!
You have made a way for me when I needed help.
PSALM 4:1

WATCHMAN NEE

(1903–72)

A SECOND CHANCE

Have you ever had something happen that changed your life? That's the type of story that can encourage others and make God famous.

Watchman Nee was born in China. His grandfather was a preacher. Watchman Nee didn't want to be like his grandfather. Following Jesus wasn't the first thing on his to-do list.

His mother, Peace Lin, started attending meetings with a speaker named Dora Yu. Watchman Nee saw a difference in his mom. He wanted to know more. He heard Dora speak, and that changed his life. He followed Jesus.

Not every story has just *one* moment when a person is completely changed. Watchman Nee went to a school in Shanghai. This was a school where students could learn from Dora Yu. This seemed perfect for Watchman Nee. He loved Jesus. But because he was lazy and often slept late, he was dismissed and sent home.

God helped Watchman Nee understand that what he did was wrong. And then God gave him a second chance. He would learn from Margaret Barber, a British missionary who took an interest in helping him.

This second chance meant Watchman Nee could become a talented writer, help people share stories of God's love, make local churches strong, and help young people know Jesus. God made this possible because a young man got a second chance, and he took it.

The last twenty years of Watchman Nee's life were spent in prison—he was arrested for his faith. But people are still encouraged to follow Jesus when they hear his story.

Like Watchman Nee, when God gives you a second chance, you should always take it!

Christ lives in me. The life I now live in this body,
I live by putting my trust in the Son of God.
GALATIANS 2:20

NEHEMIAH
(BOOK OF NEHEMIAH)

FAITHFUL IN SMALL THINGS

God has something big in mind that only you can do. Does He want you to do it right now? Maybe, but maybe not. First, God wants to see if you will do small things well. That might mean making sure you obey when a parent tells you to keep your room clean or to take out the garbage.

Nehemiah's job was making sure that what the king drank wasn't poisoned. There were more important jobs, but he kept the king safe. One day Nehemiah heard that the walls of Jerusalem had been torn down. People lived in the city, but they weren't protected. No one was even trying to rebuild. No one had enough money to do this big job. Nehemiah wanted to help.

Nehemiah prayed to God, asking that the king might help rebuild the walls. When Nehemiah asked the king, he said yes. He even paid for it. Nehemiah said, "The God of heaven will make it go well for us. So we His servants will get up and build" (Nehemiah 2:20).

When Nehemiah got to Jerusalem, the people came out of their homes and helped—even when bullies showed up to make fun of them. In less than two months, the wall around the city was rebuilt, God was honored, and those men who made fun of Nehemiah couldn't believe what had happened.

When God needs something done, He will get it done. He will always use people who did a good job with small things first. That way the big things won't seem so hard.

"Fear the Lord and be faithful to worship Him with all your heart. Think of the great things He has done for you."
1 Samuel 12:24

JOHN NEWTON

(1725–1807)

THE JOURNEY

Have you ever heard someone say, "I am not what I ought to be, I am not what I want to be, I am not what I hope to be. . . ; but still I am not what I once used to be"? John Newton was the man who said this first. This is his story.

John was a preacher and a hymn writer. That's how he is remembered. But his life was filled with sad events and bad choices. John's mom died when he was seventeen. A year later he was forced to serve in the British navy. He tried running away but was caught. He was embarrassed and in trouble. Things weren't going well for John.

It wasn't long before John worked on a ship that brought slaves from Africa. A storm near Ireland almost sank the ship. John knew something needed to change. He called out to God for help.

John read the Bible, grew in his faith, and wrote the hymn "Amazing Grace." But he needed to know God more. He would learn.

What John used to be was nothing he was proud of. *What he hoped to be* was something to look forward to. *What he wanted to be* meant that he hadn't given up on himself. *What he ought to be* meant that he had learned the difference between right and wrong. God worked on John for the rest of his life. John wanted Him to.

The good news is that God hasn't given up on you either. The Christian life is a journey. Keep walking. God will keep working.

As you have put your trust in Christ Jesus the Lord to save you from the punishment of sin, now let Him lead you in every step.
Colossians 2:6

NOAH
(GENESIS 6:8–22)

GOD'S BIG BOAT

Many years passed between the time when God said there would be a worldwide flood and when Noah helped the animals into the ark. Most people didn't do what God asked them to do, but Noah and his family obeyed and were promised safety on God's big boat.

Year after year, Noah kept building the boat. It wasn't near a lake or ocean. Noah's sons helped, but no one else thought it was a good idea—except God.

It can be hard when people make fun of you, but usually better days are coming. Noah had no relief from the people who laughed at him. They didn't seem to mind laughing at God's plan to rescue people from a flood. The Bible says that "Noah was right with God. He was without blame in his time. Noah walked with God" (Genesis 6:9).

Because Noah was a friend of God, he could be brave enough to do what God asked even when no one thought it made sense. When the rain began to fall, Noah remembered that all of God's promises were true. He knew God's plans were amazing. He could trust God to protect him. God would protect Noah's family.

The rain beat against the big boat for forty days and nights. Noah's family cared for the animals. When the time was right, everyone left the ark. They were safe. God did it—He kept His promise.

God always knows more than you do. That's why reading what His Word says can help you trust Him more.

"'I know the plans I have for you,' says the Lord, 'plans for well-being and not for trouble, to give you a future and a hope.'"
JEREMIAH 29:11

LUIS PALAU
(1934–2021)

STUDENTS WHO BECOME TEACHERS

When you say you're a disciple of Jesus, it just means that you're a student and He's teaching you good things. You can learn by reading the Bible, spending time with people who have followed Jesus longer than you have, and taking the time to study so you can share what you're learning.

Luis Palau knew what that's like. He was born in Argentina. He'd read God's Word, but he wanted to serve God. And Luis dreamed big. He came to America to attend a Christian college. When things got hard, Luis said, "Don't pray for an easier life. Pray instead to be a stronger man. . .of God."

God made Luis stronger. Then He brought Billy Graham into Luis' life. Luis worked with Billy for many years. At just the right time, Billy offered to help Luis start his own ministry. The big dream was coming true.

It has been said that Luis shared Jesus with twenty-five million people in dozens of countries. This seemed to be just what Luis was born to do. He said, "The most thrilling thing you can ever do is win someone to Christ. And it's contagious. Once you do it, you don't want to stop."

Luis not only shared the gospel, but he tried to help people in other ways. One way was very important to Luis. He found many opportunities to help people who are homeless. If people know you care, they will listen to what you say—and what Luis had to share is that Jesus could change their lives.

Be a disciple. Be a student. Be someone willing to learn. Be someone willing to share what you know. Dream big.

Teach young men to be wise.
Titus 2:6

JOHN PATON

(1824–1907)

A FATHER'S LOVE

Jesus called God "Father." He told His followers to call God "Father" too. The best example of a father will always be God.

John Paton was a missionary to the New Hebrides Islands. The people were mean to each other. And those who prayed for John often wondered if the people would hurt him. But they learned to love Jesus.

Before John ever left Scotland, he had to leave his family. His father, James, worked in a factory. John worked with his dad and watched his dad stop three times a day to pray for his family.

In the last few years of his life, John remembered the day he left home. "My dear father walked with me the first six miles of the way. His counsel and tears and heavenly conversation on that parting journey are as fresh in my heart as if it had been but yesterday; and tears are on my cheeks as freely now as then."

John had good memories of his father's love his entire life. It helped him know how to be a good father to his own children.

Not everyone has a father who lives with them. Not having a dad can be hard. It can make you sad. Be courageous. God can teach you how to be a good father when you become a parent. God wants to be a good Father to you right now. While John's dad was a great example, there has never been a better example than God. Follow Him.

"Let your light shine in front of men.
Then they will see the good things you do and
will honor your Father Who is in heaven."
MATTHEW 5:16

PAUL
(BOOK OF ACTS)

A BULLY NO MORE

If you go to school, then you've probably met a bully. Every school seems to have one. They want people to do things their way. They don't seem to mind if people get hurt by the things they say or do. They want to be important.

Paul was a bully. He also wrote more than a dozen books in the Bible. How did that happen?

To be fair, Paul wasn't a bully when he wrote the books, and that's important to remember. After Jesus rose from the dead and went back to heaven, those who followed Him started churches. A lot of people became Christians. Paul had been part of a group that wanted everyone to forget about Jesus. Paul picked on Christians. They were being hurt, and he thought he was becoming the most important person around because he kept finding Christians to punish.

Then something happened. Jesus appeared to Paul on the Damascus road and asked him why he was trying to hurt Him. The bully, Paul, knew it was Jesus and that he had been very wrong about Christians. Meeting Jesus changes things.

Paul spent the rest of his life telling people that Jesus was God's Son—that He came to live among them, died for their sin, and returned to heaven. Forgiveness and eternal life were gifts He offered to those who believed in Him.

Paul could share this message because he finally believed it himself. Paul knew that the gifts of forgiveness and eternal life were available to all.

God's love went *anywhere* to rescue *anyone*, using a man who wasn't a bully *anymore*. The next time you encounter a bully, remember that God can use bullies too!

**Whoever says he is in the light but hates
his brother is still in darkness.**
1 JOHN 2:9

ALBIE PEARSON

(1934–2023)

SWING FOR THE FENCE

You've probably never heard of Albie Pearson. He was a baseball player who retired more than fifty years ago.

Albie was short. It seemed like no one thought he could help their team win. He was offered a pair of cleats, a suitcase, and $225 a month if he could do well enough to stay on the team. He was supposed to be a pitcher, but he became an excellent hitter. A few years after being named Rookie of the Year, Albie hurt his back. He made the difficult choice to hang up his cleats, pack his suitcase, and cash his last check.

Albie was offered roles in movies and television. He often turned them down because he wasn't sure they pleased God. He performed a song that sold nearly a million records. His record company fired him when he refused to sing another song that he knew wouldn't honor God. God wasn't finished with Albie.

Albie's faith led him to become a pastor. He preached. He built orphanages in Ecuador and Zambia. He helped those who needed help. Albie explained why anyone can follow God: "He's just looking for a bunch of people to love Him and be an example in loving others." You can do that, right?

Albie followed a good God. At an age when most people choose to retire, Albie and his family started a ranch where orphan boys are taken care of. They responded to love just like you do. These boys found a home with someone who understood that God's love is better than baseball.

Do not let yourselves get tired of doing good. If we do not give up, we will get what is coming to us at the right time.
GALATIANS 6:9

OUTFIELD
ALBIE PEARSON

JAMES W. C. PENNINGTON

(1807–70)

KINDNESS FOR ALL

James Pennington was born a slave and given as a gift to a slaveholder. That doesn't seem fair, but it was the way things were done in the early 1800s. James eventually escaped, and he was given the opportunity to attend Yale University after being taught to read and write. He became a preacher, and people liked to hear him speak.

James believed slavery was wrong. He even helped raise money to send some slaves back to Africa because they wanted to go home. Freedom was important to James, but he often felt as if he would one day be captured and sent back to slavery again. He was free in New York, but he really wanted to be *forever* free.

John Hooker, a man who wanted to stop slavery, attended the church where James preached. After James told him how concerned he was, John spent time and effort raising the money needed to really make James free. James didn't think anyone should have to feel the way he felt. He spent his entire life reminding people that God sent His love to the world without checking to see where they lived, the color of their skin, or how much money they had. James knew it was as simple as "Be kind to each other. Think of the other person. Forgive other people just as God forgave you because of Christ's death on the cross" (Ephesians 4:32).

James believed that God would be honored if His kindness was offered to every single person. And today you can show God's kindness to everyone you meet!

O man, He has told you what is good. What does
the Lord ask of you but to do what is fair and to love
kindness, and to walk without pride with your God?
MICAH 6:8

PETER

(BOOKS OF MATTHEW, MARK, LUKE, JOHN, AND ACTS)

THE BEST OF INTENTIONS

Jesus had twelve disciples. Peter loved following Jesus, but he was a promise breaker. Maybe you know what that's like. Maybe you've made a promise you meant to keep but you didn't keep it. Maybe someone made a promise to you and broke it.

There was a reason Jesus was called "Master" and Peter was called a "disciple." Jesus knew Peter had a lot to learn. Jesus could teach him.

Once, Peter saw Jesus walking on water and wanted to walk out to greet Him. Jesus told Peter he could, "but when he saw the strong wind, he was afraid. He began to go down in the water. He cried out, 'Lord, save me!' At once Jesus put out His hand and took hold of him. Jesus said to Peter, 'You have so little faith! Why did you doubt?' " (Matthew 14:30–31).

That was pretty typical of Peter. He wanted to trust Jesus with everything, but he kept falling back into old habits. He seemed to speak his mind and then regret it. He kept making promises he couldn't keep.

Peter said he would never deny knowing Jesus but then denied Him three times. Peter said he would never run away, but then. . .he ran away. Jesus patiently taught Peter, the promise breaker. Jesus knew what He was doing. Peter wouldn't always be thought of that way.

Peter would be used to establish the church God had in mind for His family. Jesus kept His promises and helped Peter keep his. Aren't you glad God was patient with Peter? Aren't you glad He is patient with you?

[God said,] "I will not break My agreement,
or change what was spoken by My lips."
PSALM 89:34

ALBERT PUJOLS

(1980–)

A BETTER DREAM

You've probably thought a lot about what you want to do when you grow up. Everybody has a different dream. For Albert Pujols, that dream was to play baseball in America.

His dad played softball, and Albert watched from the stands. Albert's love for the game showed up every time he stepped up to the plate or watched from the dugout.

Albert's family left their home in the Dominican Republic and moved to the United States when he was sixteen years old. Five years later, Albert was the National League Rookie of the Year.

He has won lots of awards. He has broken many baseball records. He has been part of teams that have won the World Series. But there's something more important to Albert than baseball: *Jesus.*

Albert learned that baseball wasn't the real dream. Baseball was something Albert could do, but being a child of God was so much better.

Do you dream about doing something? Do you dream about having something more? Do you dream about going somewhere? Maybe a better dream is about being someone who knows they are loved by God.

Albert has worked very hard to make life better for children with Down syndrome. Albert also works to make life better for children in the country where he was born.

Some people believe Albert will one day be a member of the National Baseball Hall of Fame. He wants to *know God* more than *being known* by baseball fans. He is a great baseball player, but he loves God and wants to serve Him well every day of his life.

How about you?

**"The person who thinks he is important will find out
how little he is worth. The person who is not trying
to honor himself will be made important."**
MATTHEW 23:12

NABEEL QURESHI
(1983–2017)

CHASING TRUTH

Some people spend most of their lives following God and doing what He wants them to do. Some people aren't sure what to believe, so they keep looking for answers. But there are other people who actually try to prove that God doesn't exist.

Nabeel Qureshi wanted to be the one to show the world that God wasn't real. He believed there was a divine being, but it wasn't God. He spoke in colleges, trying to get people to believe what he believed, *but it wasn't truth*. Then Nabeel met David Wood. David could answer the questions Nabeel asked. David asked Nabeel questions he couldn't answer. The two men became friends. Then Nabeel became a Christian.

Nabeel's life changed after he met Jesus. "I could not put the Bible down; I literally could not. It felt as if my heart would stop beating. . .if I put it down."

Nabeel was introduced to real truth, and he spent the rest of his life introducing Jesus to people who were certain He wasn't real. Nabeel spoke at dozens of universities and wrote three books. Everything he said or wrote had to do with the real truth—God is real, and His love for you can stop any argument you might have. Psalm 119:160 says, "All of Your Word is truth, and every one of Your laws, which are always right, will last forever."

God used Nabeel to share His truth with people around the world. When Nabeel died in 2017, he knew Jesus was the truth—the way to real life.

In what ways can you share the truth of Jesus today?

"You will know the truth and the truth will make you free."
JOHN 8:32

NATE SAINT

(1923–56)

WELL DONE

God has jobs for people who preach. He has jobs for missionaries. He has jobs for people who write, play sports, and teach children. You might be surprised to know that God can use *anyone* because He has jobs for *everyone*.

Nate Saint knew how to fix airplanes. He grew up in a family that liked to dream big, fix things, and fly through the air. Nate loved Jesus but didn't think of himself as a typical missionary. Some people he worked with were translating Bibles into the languages of the people they worked with. Some shared Jesus from village to village. Nate made sure they could get there in a reliable plane.

You've read the story of missionary Jim Elliot. Nate worked with Jim and was with him when they met the Auca tribe in Ecuador—a meeting that would end in death for both men. Nate felt there was no better place for him than the mission field. He said, "May we be moved with compassion as our Lord was. May we shed tears. . .for these we have failed to bring out of darkness."

Because Nate was so connected to airplanes, it's easy to understand why he would write, "When life's flight is over, and we unload our cargo at the other end, the fellow who got rid of unnecessary weight will have the most valuable cargo to present the Lord."

The Bible says that those who did what God wanted when they were alive might hear God tell them they did a good job.

God has a job for you. Do it willingly. Do it carefully. Do it faithfully.

Always do your work well for the Lord. You know that whatever you do for Him will not be wasted.
1 CORINTHIANS 15:58

STEVE SAINT
(1951–)

WHERE TO GO FROM HERE

When someone you love dies, it can be very hard to know what to think, what to do, and how to act. Steve Saint was just five years old when his father, Nate, was killed by Auca Indians in Ecuador. He could have made the decision to be angry for the rest of his life. He could have dreamed of getting even with the people who killed his dad. He could have decided that God couldn't be trusted.

Steve made a better choice. He saw the families of the men who were killed return to the Auca Indians and share God's good news with them. These families made the hard choice to forgive the Aucas because they knew the people needed Jesus and that Jesus had said, "Love those who work against you. Do good to those who hate you" (Luke 6:27). These families chose to do good. They chose love.

When Steve was ten years old, his family also moved to live with the Auca Indians. Steve learned how to live in the jungle. He was baptized by two of the men who had killed his father. They needed Jesus—and that's just who they found.

Steve no longer lives in Ecuador, but he visits often and helps his Auca family learn new skills. He also developed a flying car that can be used to easily get from one place to the next in the jungle.

Steve's dad fixed missionary airplanes. Steve followed in his father's footsteps. He also followed in God the Father's footsteps. This is a story of faithfulness, forgiveness, and following—because God always leads.

When you find yourself in a difficult situation, remember Steve's story and choose to follow God's lead.

If a man belongs to Christ, he is a new person.
The old life is gone. New life has begun.
2 Corinthians 5:17

SAMSON
(JUDGES 13–16)

THE WEAK HERO

Samson was the world's strongest man. No one else was stronger. He could lift, carry, and pull more than anyone. Samson didn't work out in a gym. He didn't always eat the right food. He wasn't a superhero. Samson was strong because God made him strong. God made him brave.

Samson fought those who fought his family. As a judge, he made decisions for the people. In his own life, Samson often made very bad choices.

One day a pretty girl named Delilah was hired by Samson's enemies to learn how to make Samson weak. She tricked Samson into telling her his secret. God had told him that he should never cut his hair. Samson's long hair would be a sign to others that God was using him in a special way. Some might think Samson was strong because he had long hair. But the truth is Samson was strong because he obeyed God.

When Samson fell asleep, Delilah shaved off his hair. And when Samson woke up, his strength was gone. His enemies took him away and made him a slave. Not one person could rescue Samson. His strength was gone. He couldn't escape, fight, or run.

As the days passed, Samson's hair grew back. God was making him strong again. Samson remembered why he needed to obey.

Samson had grown a little older. He was blind. His enemies would never set him free. But with the new strength God had given him, he pushed against the pillars of the enemy's temple, and that temple was destroyed. God alone was to be worshiped. It was good Samson remembered.

Just like Samson, your strength and bravery come from God.

I will give thanks to the Lord with all my heart.
I will tell of all the great things You have done.
PSALM 9:1

SAMUEL

(1 AND 2 SAMUEL)

DELIVERING THE MESSAGE

Samuel was an answer to prayer. His mom, Hannah, prayed for a son, and God gave her Samuel. The young boy grew close to his mom, but one day she took Samuel to the temple because she promised to give her son back to God. She wanted this gift of a child to be used by God. And God did use Samuel. "The boy served the Lord with Eli the religious leader" (1 Samuel 2:11).

God spoke to Samuel when he was still very young. Samuel didn't recognize that it was God at first, but when Samuel knew it was God speaking, he said, "Speak, for Your servant is listening" (1 Samuel 3:10).

God kept talking to Samuel. Samuel kept growing. Samuel listened and told others about what God had said. First Samuel 3:20 says, "All Israel from Dan to Beersheba knew that Samuel had become a man of God." God used Samuel to find and appoint Israel's first two kings, Saul and David. God chose Samuel to carry His messages, and Samuel was quick to deliver them.

Samuel had to speak with courage because people did not always want to hear what God had to say. But Samuel heard God's voice and wanted people to know what God said.

You can know what God wants. God's voice can be heard today. Just read what the Bible says. They are His words, and just like Samuel, God wants you to have the courage to share them.

Hannah said, ". . .I prayed for this boy, and the Lord has given me what I asked of Him. So I have given him to the Lord. . . ." And they worshiped the Lord there.
1 Samuel 1:26–28

FRANCIS SCHAEFFER
(1912–84)

GOD OF ART

How did you learn about God? Did your mom or dad tell you? Did you learn about Him in church? Have you read books like this one?

Francis Schaeffer learned about God in a way he never expected. He read the Bible. That's right. He started at the beginning and just kept reading. He felt like he'd discovered God in a way no one else had.

This young man discovered that God created every beautiful thing on earth. God was an artist in Genesis and a poet in the Psalms. God enjoyed His creation, and that caused Francis to say, "With truth comes beauty and with this beauty a freedom before God."

Francis became a preacher who loved art. He was certain there were things man could make that weren't honoring to God, but he said, "A work of art is a work of creativity, and creativity has value because God is the Creator."

He thought it was important to spend time with his children taking them to art exhibits and answering their questions about the world God made.

Others noticed his choice always to include God in what he said. Preachers also began making sure they read God's Word carefully before they tried to share what God thought on all kinds of issues.

Not every work of art honors God, but all art shows that mankind seeks beautiful things because God created beauty.

What is your favorite thing in creation?

Let the heavens be glad. And let the earth be full of joy. Let the sea and all that is in it make a loud noise. Let the fields and all that is in them be full of joy. Then all the trees of the land will sing for joy.
PSALM 96:11–12

SHADRACH, MESHACH, AND ABEDNEGO

(DANIEL 3)

BRAVERY IN THE BLAZE

Music is an important part of musical chairs. When the music plays, you walk around the chairs; and when the music stops, you hurry to find a seat. If you can't find one, you're out of the game.

The Bible tells a story of three young men—Shadrach, Meshach, and Abednego. They were all born in Israel and followed the honest and for real God. When these men were young, they were captured and brought to Babylon. The people there didn't follow God. They made their own rules, like the time the Babylonian king Nebuchadnezzar came up with a law that sounded a lot like musical chairs.

The king had a large idol made. He said the people would need to bow down to it whenever the musicians in his kingdom started playing music. When the music stopped, everyone could go back to what they were doing. If you didn't bow, it was game over for you.

Shadrach, Meshach, and Abednego wouldn't bow. The king thought they might have misunderstood his law, so he gave them a second chance—but the three men still refused. This made the king mad. He had a large furnace, and he made sure it was seven times hotter than usual. He had his soldiers throw the three men into the fire. But they didn't die, burn, or cry, because God was with them in the fire and saved them.

Finally, King Nebuchadnezzar did the right thing. He honored God—and he told the three to come out of the flames. They may have worked for a king, but they served God.

Just like Shadrach, Meshach, and Abednego, when you serve God, you can be brave and stand up for what's right.

[God said,] "I will honor those who honor Me.
And those who hate Me will not be honored."
1 SAMUEL 2:30

KYLE SNYDER

(1995–)

WRESTLING WITH GRATITUDE

Some people are so successful that it's hard to list everything they've done. Kyle Snyder is one of those people. He's one amazing wrestler. If we were to look at every title and match he has won from high school through college and then look at his performance in the Olympics, we wouldn't have much room to talk about anything else.

Something sets Kyle apart from other wrestlers—and it's not just that he's really good. Once when Kyle participated in a wrestling match at a competitor's school, a school worker did his best to make sure each wrestler had enough water to drink when his match was over. Kyle was the only one who thanked the man for his thoughtfulness. He thanked him more than once.

Was Kyle a thoughtful young man? Sure. Did he come from a kind family? Yes. Did he go to church? He did. But there was more to it than that.

Kyle became a Christian in high school, and he allowed God to redirect his choices. That meant that he chose to work hard and show thankfulness.

Good things will happen. Bad things will happen. Be grateful that God has a plan for everything that will ever happen.

Kyle may understand gratitude more than most. He certainly is a good example. Ephesians 5:4 says, "Do not be guilty of telling bad stories and of foolish talk. These things are not for you to do. Instead, you are to give thanks for what God has done for you." Be courageous—say thanks.

Let the peace of Christ have power over your hearts.
You were chosen as a part of His body. Always be thankful.
COLOSSIANS 3:15

SOLOMON
(1 KINGS 3)

A GIFT FOR THE KING

If God asked you what gift you would like more than any other gift, what would it be? Would you ask for money? Fame? Special abilities? When Solomon was made king, God asked him what gift he wanted.

Solomon could have asked for many gifts, but for him the decision was easy. If he was going to lead so many people, he would need wisdom. First Kings 4:29 says, "God gave Solomon wisdom and much understanding and learning, as much as the sand beside the sea."

That wisdom was useful. One day two women came to the new king. They both had babies, but in the night one of the babies died. Each woman said that the baby that was left was her child. God wants moms to love their children. Most moms do. King Solomon wanted to see who loved the baby more. Wisdom said that the woman who wanted the child to live was the real mom.

Solomon offered to give half of the baby to one mom and the other half to the second mom. Solomon had no intention of harming the baby, but one woman thought his idea was good; the other said the baby should live. When he heard what the women said, Solomon knew that the real mom would want her baby to live. He gave the baby to her. People were amazed by their new king's wisdom.

Do you want to be wise? God's wisdom is always found in the pages of His Word.

If you do not have wisdom, ask God for it. He is always ready
to give it to you and will never say you are wrong for asking.
JAMES 1:5

CHARLES SPURGEON

(1834–92)

IT STARTED WITH A SNOWSTORM

God can use anything to cause people who need rescue to notice Him. Some people hear a song that makes them think about God for the first time. Friends can help friends notice God. For Charles Spurgeon, it was a verse. In Isaiah 45:22, God said, "Look to Me and be saved, all the ends of the earth. For I am God, and there is no other."

Charles heard a sermon when that verse was spoken. He might not have heard that verse when he did if a snowstorm hadn't stopped him from traveling. Charles preached his first sermon within a year of beginning his journey with Jesus. Within four years, he was a preacher. By the age of twenty-two, he was the most popular preacher anyone knew.

When people sinned, Charles reminded them that "God is more ready to forgive me than I am ready to [sin]." When they wondered how to grow in Jesus, he said, "Bible study is the metal that makes a Christian. This is the strong meat on which holy men are nourished." When they wondered if God would do what He said, Charles responded, "[You can't] out-believe God. God never out-promised Himself."

God gave Charles a great gift. He could preach, write, and care deeply for people. Charles had to remember that the message he shared was not his but God's. Charles' job wasn't to impress people by how well he could speak but rather to make sure he delivered a message that God sent through His Word.

God can get your attention with a snowstorm or a Bible verse or something else. In what ways has God gotten your attention?

I am not ashamed of the Good News. It is the power of
God. It is the way He saves men from the punishment
of their sins if they put their trust in Him.
ROMANS 1:16

JOHN STAM

(1907–34)

JUST BEFORE CHRISTMAS

Not every story is happy. Bad things happen to people every day. Understanding why can be hard.

John Stam followed Jesus—all the way to China as a missionary. His wife, Betty, lived in China. She was the daughter of Chinese missionaries. Together they started their ministry. Together they shared God's good news. Together they had a daughter named Helen.

Early in December 1934, John and Betty looked forward to Helen's first Christmas. That's when the young family was surprised, and not in a good way. Members of the Red Army came into their home, demanded their money, and kidnapped them.

They were taken to the city jail. A note was discovered that included a verse that showed John was ready to live or die. Philippians 1:20 says, "I hope very much that I will have no reason to be ashamed. I hope to honor Christ with my body if it be by my life or by my death. I want to honor Him without fear, now and always."

John's note never made it out of China. John and Betty never returned home. Two days later, the soldiers killed the missionary couple. Betty had hidden their daughter, Helen. She was later rescued.

A story like John's is sad, but it has encouraged many people over many years to become missionaries and serve God with "no reason to be ashamed." God always gets the last word, and He stands with those who hurt. Psalm 34:18 says that God "is near to those who have a broken heart. And He saves those who are broken in spirit."

How can John's story encourage you?

"What does a man have if he gets all the world and loses his own soul? What can a man give to buy back his soul?"
MATTHEW 16:26

BILLY SUNDAY

(1862–1935)

FEELING UNACCEPTABLE

When you feel unsure of yourself, unacceptable, or when you think you won't amount to much, think of Billy Sunday.

Billy was born into a poor family, and his dad died just a few weeks after he was born. His mom tried to make a life for her family but eventually sent Billy to an orphanage.

There Billy discovered that he loved baseball. When he was eighteen years old, he moved to Marshalltown, Iowa, because they needed a baseball player for their fire brigade baseball team. Two years later, Billy helped them win the state championship.

Billy moved on to the major leagues. He played for eight seasons with three different teams, starting in Chicago.

At times Billy felt insecure. When he played in Chicago, he heard a small band playing a hymn his mother had sung when he was young. He moved closer to listen. It wasn't long before Billy became a Christian. Maybe this memory is why Billy said, "There is nothing in the world of art like the songs Mother used to sing."

Billy moved from catching baseballs to preaching God's good news. For years Billy traveled, preaching to anyone who would listen. The crowds grew large. It's been said that more than a million people came to know Jesus because Billy shared God's love. Even with so many good things happening, Billy sometimes felt abandoned and unacceptable. So God helped Billy's wife, Nell, be the encouragement he needed.

The hardest thing for some people to believe is that God loves them, accepts them, and made them to be His children. You can be sure of those things when you feel unsure about everything else.

There is no fear in love. Perfect love puts fear out of our hearts.
1 John 4:18

HUDSON TAYLOR
(1832–1905)

WE ARE WEAK, BUT HE IS STRONG

This is a story of the power of a godly example. Having a godly example is very important. Being one is just as important.

Hudson Taylor started China Inland Missions, and more than eight hundred missionaries went to China because of Hudson's example. He spent more than fifty years working in China. As with most missionaries, life was hard for Hudson, but he had learned that "there are three stages to every great work of God; first it is impossible, then it is difficult, then it is done."

You've read the story of George Müller. It was George who influenced Hudson to pray for God's help before asking anyone else for help. You've read the story of Charles Spurgeon. It was Charles who encouraged Hudson never to give up. You've read the stories of Jim Elliot, Billy Graham, and Luis Palau. Each has said that he was influenced by the life and ministry of Hudson Taylor.

The choices you make can be influenced by others and can impact the lives of even more. Remember this on your worst days: "When I cannot read, when I cannot think, when I cannot even pray, I can trust." Hudson said those words.

When life is hard, trust God. Hudson trusted Him to open doors for ministry in China, and eighteen thousand people came to know Jesus. In many ways, Hudson changed the way people thought of missionary work when he said, "God uses men who are weak. . .enough to lean on Him."

Lean hard. God is *always* strong enough.

Faith is being sure we will get what we hope for.
It is being sure of what we cannot see.
HEBREWS 11:1

ROBERT PRESTON TAYLOR

(1909–97)

PRISONER OF WAR

Robert Preston Taylor was a chaplain. That means he was a pastor for soldiers. He was a member of the air force and helped soldiers with their faith.

Robert served as chaplain during World War II but was taken captive when American forces surrendered to the Japanese. He walked in the Bataan Death March, as Japanese soldiers moved more than fifty thousand American soldiers to a camp for prisoners of war. Many soldiers died.

The Japanese allowed Robert to continue sharing God's love with soldiers, and he ministered to thousands of men in the hospital. But Robert was put in solitary confinement (kept away from other prisoners) for trying to get food and medicine to soldiers in the hospital. He spent fourteen weeks away from those who needed him.

Robert spent more than three years as a prisoner of war, but he never pushed God away even when it would have been easy to give up. Robert said, "In the prison camp you live one day at a time but with your eye on the future. . .with. . .hope and faith."

In 1945 the war was over. Rescue arrived. Looking back on those days, Robert said, "The key to all of it, though, was. . .God, but in His good way we were able to be optimistic and to keep on. . . , not only for yourself but for those about you."

When hard times come, trust God to give you hope and strength—no matter what happens.

We know that troubles help us learn not to give up. When we have learned not to give up, it shows we have stood the test. When we have stood the test, it gives us hope. Hope never makes us ashamed because the love of God has come into our hearts through the Holy Spirit Who was given to us.

ROMANS 5:3–5

TIM TEBOW

(1987–)

ALL HEART

How frustrating would it be to prove you are really good at something and then be told by someone that you're not needed? Would you have a bad attitude? Would you want to tell them they're wrong?

Tim Tebow knows how that feels. He was a fantastic football player in high school. He was an amazing football player in college. He proved he could play football in the National Football League, but he was let go from one team and then another. Pretty soon no team wanted to hire Tim.

Baseball was also one of Tim's favorite sports, so he tried that. He hasn't made the major leagues, but he has played on some AA teams. His first at bat was a home run, but he has been injured, and he doesn't always hit home runs.

It's rare to see Tim upset. He continues to work hard because he wants to please his Boss. Tim has followed Jesus for many years, and he's quick to admit that he wants to do what Jesus wants him to do. When he's not on the field, he might be serving God in other ways. He has given and helped raise money for an orphanage, a hospital, disadvantaged kids, and kids with cancer.

If Tim's job changes, he can remember what God said in Colossians 3:24: "Remember that you will get your reward from the Lord. He will give you what you should receive. You are working for the Lord Christ."

When you work for God, He gets to choose what you do—and you'll enjoy it a lot more. He'll also help you do it!

I can do all things because Christ gives me the strength.
PHILIPPIANS 4:13

WILLIAM TYNDALE

(1494–1536)

DISCOVERING THE BIBLE

Do you remember the story of King Josiah? He read God's Word after it had been hidden for many years. Josiah wanted to do what God actually asked. He didn't want anyone to guess.

William Tyndale's story is a lot like Josiah's. He learned how to speak and read Greek so he could read the original words of the Bible. He read things in the original Greek language that were different than things most people learned in church. He believed everyone should know what God actually said. He didn't think anyone should guess.

That got William into trouble. Maybe it was because those who preached didn't want to be proven wrong. Maybe they didn't want to change what they taught. Maybe they thought William was trying to make them look bad. William knew that helping people read God's Word was something he had to do. Joshua 1:8 says, "This book of the Law must not leave your mouth. Think about it day and night, so you may be careful to do all that is written in it."

If what William was learning was important to God, it should be important to everyone who believed in God.

William took time to take the original Greek words and make them understandable in English. He was told to stop, but William kept working. One day William was captured and later killed for writing down the Bible in English.

It was William's work that made English-language Bibles possible. His work is what allows you to read the Bible today!

Everything that was written in the Holy Writings
long ago was written to teach us. By not giving
up, God's Word gives us strength and hope.
ROMANS 15:4

CARSON WENTZ

(1992–)

GOOD FRIENDS

Do you have a best friend? When did you meet him or her? Were you friends right away? What makes that person such a good friend? Having a good friend is a pretty cool thing.

Carson Wentz would agree. He was accepted into the National Football League as one of the best new players in 2016. He beat plenty of records and was named Rookie of the Year.

Sometimes when you become famous, it's hard to have friends who aren't just fans. That's the kind of friend Carson needed, and it's the kind of friend he found. He became friends with Mike Trout, who just happens to be a major-league baseball player, and he's pretty talented too. Mike was also a Rookie of the Year in 2012.

Both men are easygoing and love the outdoors, and they're both Christians. The encouragement they give each other is important to both of them. They know that good friendships are important to God. First Corinthians 15:33 says, "Do not let anyone fool you. Bad people can make those who want to live good become bad."

The two men work several thousand miles from each other, but their friendship seems stronger than distance.

Carson started the AO1 Foundation, which feeds people in need, helps the disadvantaged to enjoy outdoor experiences, and has helped to develop a sports complex in Haiti. AO1 stands for an Audience of One. Carson does what he does because he loves Jesus and has friends like Mike who support him.

Do you have a friend who supports you like that?

**Love each other as Christian brothers. Show respect
for each other. Do not be lazy but always work hard.
Work for the Lord with a heart full of love for Him.**
ROMANS 12:10–11

JOHN WESLEY

(1703–91)

BEST OF ALL, GOD IS WITH YOU

You probably know more about Jesus today than last year. As a Christian, you're being made into a new creation. Things that you think and believe change as you learn more about Jesus.

That happened to John Wesley. Raised in a large family, John is known for his preaching and writing. Even John needed to change the things he thought and believed as he was made new.

John and a few friends formed a club that mean people called "The Holy Club" as an insult. The young men who were part of this group spent at least three hours every night learning what they could from the Bible. They tried to pray every hour of the day. They went without food twice a week, visited prisoners, and helped take care of sick people.

Very few of the young men could keep up with all the things the group was trying to do. They weren't enjoying their friendship with God. They were too tired.

Over the years, John learned that God's rescue plan didn't need help. Titus 3:4–5 says, "But God, the One Who saves, showed how kind He was and how He loved us by saving us from the punishment of sin. It was not because we worked to be right with God. It was because of His loving-kindness that He washed our sins away."

This was the kind of changed thinking that helped John reach out to so many people during his life. Read the verse from Titus 3 again, and remember, you serve a big God, and best of all, He is with you.

The saving of those who are right with God is from
the Lord. He is their strength in time of trouble.
PSALM 37:39

GEORGE WHITEFIELD
(1714–70)

BECOMING APPROACHABLE

Maybe you go to a church that uses drama to help you understand what the preacher will say. George Whitefield would have wanted to visit your church. He probably would have felt at home.

When George started his ministry, he didn't preach in church buildings. Most of his sermons were given outside—usually in a farmer's field. He often used drama.

George became friends with Ben Franklin. They didn't always agree, but Ben thought George was very good at making sure people understood his message and had the chance to follow God. Ben believed George could preach to as many as thirty thousand people at one time. That's saying something special. There were no microphones when George was alive. He must have had a very powerful voice.

George thought slaves should be treated with respect. He often preached sermons to the slaves in the towns he visited.

While some people thought George was too harsh, others said he was more approachable the older he got. God did the same for Paul, who wrote in Colossians 4:6, "Speak with them in such a way they will want to listen to you. Do not let your talk sound foolish. Know how to give the right answer to anyone."

After many years of preaching, George died. His friend John Wesley preached at his funeral. Friends were important to George.

No one gets to where God wants them to go without traveling companions. God brought friends into George's life who helped him become more like the man God made him to be. He will bring friends like that into your life too.

One man is able to have power over him who is
alone, but two can stand against him. It is not
easy to break a rope made of three strings.
ECCLESIASTES 4:12

WILLIAM WILBERFORCE

(1759–1833)

HE DIDN'T BACK DOWN

You might go to church because it's a family thing to do. Maybe you're interested in Jesus because someone you know talks about Him. You may not know what to think.

William Wilberforce grew up in a family that loved Jesus. William learned about Jesus but never really followed Him as a child. He was confused about the things he was told, and he liked making bad choices.

As a young man, William was involved in British politics. He soon realized that he needed to know Jesus, and that's when he began his lifelong journey.

Many members of Parliament thought that being a Christian made a person unfit for politics. They made fun of William and wanted him to leave. He didn't. He actually relied on his new love for Jesus to help him stand up for truth, the poor, and freeing slaves.

William helped stop the slave trade in England. It didn't happen overnight. Many years would pass before William saw real change.

William wanted to follow God's Word. He once said, "What a difference it would be if our system of morality were based on the Bible."

You've read the story of John Newton. He wrote the hymn "Amazing Grace." John told William that he should continue to fight to free slaves. Both men were changed by God's love, and they were certain everyone deserved the chance to be free. They waited most of their lives to see that day.

What do *you* stand for?

Let God change your life. First of all, let Him give you a
new mind. Then you will know what God wants you to do.
And the things you do will be good and pleasing and perfect.
ROMANS 12:2

JOHN WYCLIFFE

(C. 1320–84)

KNOW THE TRUTH

Before William Tyndale was born, there was John Wycliffe. William thought it was important for people to be able to read what God had to say in their own language. That's what John believed too.

When religious leaders wanted to know why this was so important to John, he said, "All Christian life is to be measured by Scripture; by every word." *People needed to read it.*

When those same religious leaders refused to admit that what they taught was not found in the Bible, John said, "I believe that in the end the truth will conquer." *God's Word is truth.*

When they argued that the people didn't need scripture in their language, John said, "Believers should have the Scriptures in a language familiar to the people." *People needed to understand it.*

John was threatened and told to be quiet. Jesus faced something like this when He spoke about religious leaders called Pharisees. Jesus said, "They like to have the important places at big suppers and the best seats in the Jewish places of worship. They like to have people show respect to them as they stand in the center of town where people gather. They like to be called teacher" (Matthew 23:6–7).

Because God gave the words in the Bible, it's important to know and understand them. This was important to John Wycliffe and William Tyndale. It was important to Jesus. It should be important to you too.

The Word of the Lord is worth more than gold, even more
than much fine gold. They are sweeter than honey, even
honey straight from the comb. And by them Your servant is
told to be careful. In obeying them there is great reward.
PSALM 19:10–11

BROTHER YUN
(1958–)

WEAK MAN, STRONG GOD

Would it be hard to live in a place where you were punished for loving God? What if you were told you couldn't pray? How would you feel if God was outlawed?

Liu Zhenying was born in China. His story is encouraging. Today most people call Liu "Brother Yun."

Yun's becoming a Christian was not a popular decision. The police visited him and told him to change his mind. But becoming a Christian was the only thing that gave Yun hope.

He believed in God, trusted Jesus, and learned from God's Spirit. People didn't think he was important, but God had important things for Yun to do. Yun said, "It is not great men who change the world, but weak men in the hands of a great God."

Yun was happy to be weak if it meant God would be strong. Yun needed help. He was put in prison, beaten, and made to live without food for many days. But God had good plans for Yun's prison days. Prison guards watched how Yun lived through hard times. He shared his faith, and prisoners and guards believed what he said. Many followed Jesus.

Proverbs 19:21 says, "There are many plans in a man's heart, but it is the Lord's plan that will stand." For Yun, God's plan included sending missionaries from China to nearby countries so even more people could know the difference God makes.

Yun thought of himself as weak. A strong God can use that kind of man. God can use that kind of boy too!

We will follow the plan of the work He has given us to do.
2 Corinthians 10:13

LOUIS ZAMPERINI

(1917–2014)

THE FORGIVEN FORGAVE

God forgave you. He says it's important to forgive others. The ones who hurt you? *Yes!* The ones who should know better? *Yes!* The ones who didn't ask for forgiveness? *Forgive them all!*

Good things were happening for Louis Zamperini. As a young man, he learned to run, and he broke records. He ran in the Olympics in Berlin in 1936. His family was poor, but Louis' successes made him think his life was going to be much easier.

In the 1940s, Louis fought in World War II. An airplane he was in went down. For more than forty days, he floated on the ocean hoping to be rescued. He landed on a small island, but Japanese soldiers made him a prisoner. He was tortured for a long time.

Louis didn't like his captors; in fact, he hated them. He wanted to do anything he could to pay them back. About four years after he returned home, Louis attended a Billy Graham crusade and became a Christian. He discovered something valuable: "The hardest thing in life is to forgive. Hate is self-destructive. If you hate somebody, you're not hurting the person you hate, you're hurting yourself."

Jesus said that one of the best ways to pray includes forgiveness. Luke 11:4 says, "Forgive us our sins, as we forgive those who sin against us."

Louis spent the rest of his life telling people about Jesus and forgiving the men who hurt him during the war.

Who do you need to forgive?

When someone does something bad to you, do not do the same thing to him. When someone talks about you, do not talk about him. Instead, pray that good will come to him.
1 Peter 3:9

CHECK OUT THIS FUN FAITH MAP!

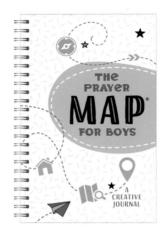

The Prayer Map for Boys
978-1-68322-558-4

This prayer journal is a fun and creative way to fully experience the power of prayer. Each page guides you to write out thoughts, ideas, and lists. . .creating a specific "map" for you to follow as you talk to God. Each map includes a spot to record the date, so you can look back on your prayers and see how God has worked in your life.

Spiral Bound